Sir Kenneth Bloomfield was born in Belfast in 1931, and educated at the Royal Belfast Academical Institution ("Inst"), where he is now chairman of the Board of Governors, and St Peter's College, Oxford, of which he is now an Honorary Fellow, and from which he graduated in Modern History.

He entered the Northern Ireland Civil Service in 1952, becoming Permanent Secretary to the "power-sharing Executive" in 1974, followed by terms as the official head of the Environment and Economic Development Departments. His civil service career culminated in his appointment to be Head of the Service from 1984 to 1991.

Since leaving the civil service, Sir Kenneth has held an extraordinary range of public and private sector appointments. He has been the founding chairman of the Chief Executives Forum, the Northern Ireland Higher Education Council and the Northern Ireland Legal Services Commission, the Northern Ireland National Governor of the BBC, vice chairman of the National Museum and Galleries, a board member of the Green Park Healthcare Trust, Opera Northern Ireland, a senator of Queen's University, Victims Commissioner, chairman of the review of Criminal Injuries Compensation and co-commissioner of the Independent Commission for the Location of Victims' Remains. In recent years, as chairman of the Association for Quality Education, he has been a spokesman for grammar schools seeking to preserve academic selection.

He has also worked outside Northern Ireland, both in Great Britain and further afield. At the national level, he was involved in a review of the top structure of the Department of Social Security and an inquiry into the pay of NHS dentists. He served on a body set up by the General Synod of the Church of England to review the system for the appointment of bishops. He was appointed by the States of Jersey, the island parliament, to a body reviewing its system of government. His involvement in the issue of victims of terrorism has taken him to Israel, Austria and the Netherlands. He has also worked as a short-term consultant in Bangladesh.

Sir Kenneth is a published author. In addition to many articles, he produced in 1994 a memoir, *Stormont in Crisis*, which dealt with his life up to 1991, and his 1998 report on victims, *We Will Remember Them*, has been translated into Castillian and Basque.

He is an Honorary Doctor of Queen's University, the University of Ulster and the Open University, a recipient of the Ben Wilson trophy for Individual or Corporate Excellence and a Select Preacher at Oxford University.

He and his wife Elizabeth, both survivors of a bomb attack on their Crawfordsburn home in 1988, have two children, Caroline and Timothy, both married. Elizabeth has been active in the pursuit of many good causes.

A NEW LIFE

For my good friend and colleague Eric

A NEW LIFE

KENNETH BLOOMFIELD

Ken. Bloomfield

June '08

THE BREHON PRESS
BELFAST

First published 2008 by
The Brehon Press Ltd
1A Bryson Street
Belfast BT5 4ES
Northern Ireland

ISBN: 978 1 905474 26 4

Cover design by Jake Campbell
Printed and bound by J.H. Haynes & Co Ltd

for Elizabeth, Caroline and Timothy

CONTENTS

Prologue

IN ONE OF THOSE HIGH-PROFILE, BUT ultimately useless
initiatives associated with the premiership of the late Harold
Wilson, the government of the day introduced in tandem a
Selective Employment Tax coupled with a Selective Employment
Premium for those involved in manufacturing industry. The
reputed midwives of this complex fiscal initiative were, it was
alleged, the émigré economists, Messrs Ballogh and Kaldor.
Those who were unimpressed were heard to say that "perhaps it
made sense before it was translated from the original
Hungarian". It was even suggested that, to take advantage of
the new fiscal regime, the Prince of Wales might change his
historic motto, "Ich dien", or "I serve", to "I manufacture."

Yet it was Margaret Thatcher, above all, who was to make
those involved in public service, whether paid or unpaid, feel
that they were deemed of less value to society and the economy
than the so-called "wealth creators". There was, somehow, the
impression that only the cautious and second-rate would opt for
the haven of public service rather than the choppy waters of
bracing competition.

The end of her tenancy—one might almost say her reign—at
10 Downing Street occurred not long before my own retirement

on 15 April 1991, from the lesser but not always undemanding post of Head of the Northern Ireland Civil Service. If I did not share much else with that formidable Prime Minister, I did share the experience of emerging intact from a well-planned attempt to assassinate me.

When, in 1994, I published a memoir, *Stormont in Crisis*, it was inevitably much concerned with my career as a public official in challenging times. The final words of the book describe my departure from the Stormont stage at the conclusion of a farewell reception in the Great Hall. As I wrote then: "The photographs were taken; the last hands were shaken; we walked through the Great Hall and down the steps, and drove off to a new life."

That "new life" has proved to be unexpectedly interesting, challenging and varied. In this account of it I hope to show that useful life need not end at the statutory retirement age, whatever it may be; that one can, if both willing and fortunate, participate in extraordinarily diverse activities. As I begin to write this, my wife Elizabeth and I have just returned from Buckingham Palace where we attended one of the events held to mark the year of the Queen's eightieth birthday. We were invited, as explained in a rather grand invitation from the Master of the Household, as people over sixty continuing to play a significant part in the national life. Dear Elizabeth, my companion and stay for more than forty-five years, did not attend simply as my consort but as someone who has, year after year, worked for innumerable good causes. We were in fascinating company: Dame Mary Peters, Olympic Gold Medallist, Sir James Galway, magical flautist, Gloria Hunniford, enduring television personality, with others from our native Northern Ireland; and countless others immediately recognisable—Rolf Harris, Michael Parkinson, Bobby Charlton, Jonathan Dimbleby, Stephen Hawking. All of them could tell interesting stories, and point to fascinating and busy lives. For myself, I can now look back with pleasure at that "new life" which awaited us as I walked down those Stormont steps.

1

Towards Better Government

ONE OF MY HIGHEST PRIORITIES IN my final years in government had been to improve conditions in the most deprived areas of Belfast through a programme called "Making Belfast Work". To achieve our ends, it was essential for a wide range of government departments and other public bodies not merely to acknowledge this new priority but to work effectively together in doing so. I probably wearied some of my colleagues by my constant reminder to them that, while fine pieces of music were written for and performed by solo instruments, the grandest music of all was produced by the full range of instruments playing together as an orchestra, with each making its distinctive contribution to a single score.

In recent years we have disturbing evidence that, even within a single government department, there can be appalling failures to communicate and cooperate effectively. The events leading to the resignation of Charles Clarke as Home Secretary showed all too clearly the danger of narrow focus and an inability to take in the bigger picture.

Two much-vaunted "reforms" during the later part of my civil service career had, in my view, made the situation worse rather than better. A new emphasis on "performance pay" failed to acknowledge sufficiently a wholesome tradition of team-working. An individual knowing he would be judged, and his remuneration affected, by his or her delivery of certain defined results or "targets" would tend to stick to his own last. The so-called "Next Steps" initiative led to the widespread creation of "executive agencies", distanced to some extent from the policy-making core of departments. It was not a wholly new idea. In the Irish Republic the so-called Devlin Report had advanced a similar argument years before. Moreover, although the term itself had not yet been invented, the creation of a Northern Ireland Housing Executive in the Seventies had brought about precisely this separation between the parent department—with its control of broad policy, legislative change and funding—and the executive responsible for delivering house-building and management on the ground. I had found myself at the sharp end of this relationship as Permanent Secretary of the Northern Ireland Department of the Environment. I had a reservation that policy formed without direct experience of executive action could be unrealistic; that executive action could drift away from the main purpose of public policy. I shall have more to say about the role of the "executive agency" later.

At the centre of the public system in Northern Ireland the permanent heads of the several government departments met regularly, and were frequently able to identify or iron-out problems in new policies before ministers needed to be involved. We had to remember, though, that while the Northern Ireland Civil Service, then employing some 28,000 people, represented an important part of the wider public service, it was greatly outnumbered by colleagues elsewhere in the public sector; in the health and education services, in local government, in an array of non-departmental public bodies and elsewhere. The Civil Service itself was so large in a province of some 1.6 million people because it embodied many functions performed elsewhere by local government or other bodies.

When Northern Ireland had degenerated into serious disorder

and James Callaghan as Home Secretary had become heavily involved, several "working parties" on aspects of the situation, involving both Stormont and Whitehall officials, had been established by the Stormont government after a suggestion not dissimilar to an order from Callaghan. Aficionados of *The Godfather* would have recognised it at once as "an offer you can't refuse". Some consideration was given at that time to embodying public servants into a wider Public Service, but this was seen to be "a bridge too far". Local authorities, in particular, were bound to defend to the death their right to remain the employers of their own officials.

It was not, therefore, the case that senior officials across the whole public sector met regularly to discuss common problems and opportunities. Each department was like a separate planet in contact with its own moons; the Department of Health with health boards, the Department of Education with education boards, and so on. Yet it was clear that the whole universe of public service faced many common problems, for example, in taking appropriate action to ensure employment equality.

The only organisation to occupy this vacuum was a body called the Public Service Training Council (PSTC), led by a visionary enthusiast called Jim Maguire. It was his initiative to hold an annual event for chief officers across the public sector, to which major figures such as Heads of the Home Civil Service or Professors from the Wharton School would come as speakers from time to time. But the real business tended to be done, not at the formal seminars, but in the bar of the Slieve Donard Hotel. Jim was one of that numerous band who are prophets other than in their home country. Towards the end of my Civil Service career I travelled with him to Sweden and Finland to discuss civil service organisation, management and training in those progressive countries, and found that my companion—already terribly ill and with only a short time to live—was held in the highest esteem in those countries.

In a changing world it seemed ridiculous that the dialogue

across the public sector should depend upon conversations at an annual event and so we began to develop an idea of a "club" or "voluntary cooperative", to which every chief executive of a public body, large or small, executive or advisory, could belong. So the blue-print for a Chief Executives' Forum was drawn up, with much invaluable help from Professor Sean Fulton of the Queen's University Belfast, and I was asked to become its first Chairman on my retirement from the Civil Service in 1991.

We had the great good fortune to obtain as our Chief Executive, on secondment from the Housing Executive, a certain Alvin McKinley, whose support for me and my successors in the chair, and rare enthusiasm and insight have been paramount factors in the organisation's progress and success. Initially funded by the Department of Finance, subsequently drawing financial support from member organisations, and ultimately "floated off" to be self-supporting, the Forum has won the respect of the wider public sector. Over the years our membership grew steadily, both because of the services we provided and because new public bodies came into being. To guide the development of our programme, I formed a Core Group of "heavy hitters" from the Civil Service and other public services. We looked to our membership to identify issues of common concern for discussion at conferences and seminars. One of the most interesting developments was the more or less spontaneous emergence of sub-groups focussing on a special interest. There were not, in those early and more backward days, all that many female chief executives in the Northern Ireland public sector, and some years would pass before the appointment of the first woman Permanent Secretary, but quite early in the life of the Forum, our female members decided to meet regularly as a sub-group.

It also became clear that there was a huge difference between leading a public body with a budget of many millions, a staff numbered in thousands, and the means to deploy a wide range of legal, financial, personnel, technological and other expert professionals, or on the other hand, leading a much smaller body with (perhaps) fewer than twenty staff, but still bearing the responsibility of being a subordinate Accounting Officer, liable to censure by the Public Accounts Committee if things went badly wrong. This loneliness of ultimate responsibility, without extensive support, motivated the chief officers concerned to form a Smaller Public Bodies sub-group within which they could advise and mutually support each other.

Across the United Kingdom, the public sector spends every year enormous sums in employing McKinsey or Capita and other prestigious consultants. Part of this, I fear, flows from the wish to be able to say when under criticism, "I took the best possible advice." Yet the public sector itself is a vast reservoir of knowledge and experience. How stupid it would be to spend taxpayers' money looking for a solution which had already been tried and tested by a colleague in another organisation.

Perhaps the most interesting initiative taken by the Forum during my term as its first Chairman was the publication, in partnership with the Joseph Rowntree Foundation, of a book of essays entitled *People and Government: Questions for Northern Ireland*. Around that time, and after years of violence and instability, minds were beginning to turn to the vital question of how Northern Ireland might be governed in more peaceful and stable times. Politicians and political scientists were having their say but we had, within our own membership, people of great and varied experience. I discussed the idea of such a publication with Sir Charles Carter, as representing the Foundation. Charles had been a professor at Queen's, Chairman of the Northern Ireland Economic Council, and Vice Chancellor at Lancaster University. He and I agreed to act as joint editors, and to commission a series of relevant essays from public servants and others. I used a chairman's privilege to contribute two essays rather than one. In the first of these I examined the distribution of powers and responsibilities between government departments in Northern Ireland. I argued that lines of responsibility needed to be clear and widely understood; and that future arrangements should promote intra-sector and inter-sector cooperation.

My second theme arose out of the emphatic assertion at that time by unionist parties that they would never contemplate a return to the kind of "power-sharing executive" which had risen and fallen in 1974. (Later events were to justify Seamus Mallon's description of the Good Friday Agreement as "Sunningdale for slow learners.") I could see no prospect of any return to single-party government and, if ingenious forms of coalition government were ruled out, was there any alternative?

In thinking about this, I recalled that Jersey in the Channel Islands conducted its government not through a cabinet of ministers, but through a system of committees. I remembered too those far-off days in the Sixties when Professor Tom Wilson had drawn up Northern Ireland's first ever Economic Plan with the support of a small but gifted team, including a young Cambridge economist, Colin Powell. Later Colin had been attracted to work for the States (or parliament) of Jersey, first of all as their Chief Economic Adviser, and later as their Chief Adviser and the acknowledged leading public official in that jurisdiction. So it was that I wrote to Colin asking if I might pay a short visit to the island to see how its system of government worked. In due course I arrived at St Helier Airport to be picked up by an official with the splendid title of Greffier. In a busy couple of days Colin enabled me to meet all the movers and shakers of the island, up to and including the Bailiff himself, who manages to be chief citizen, Speaker of the island's legislative assembly and Chief Justice of the Royal Court, all in one. On my return I wrote an essay on my impressions of the Jersey system, within which the President of the influential Policy and Resources Committee had some ability to encourage coordination, but nothing approaching the power of a Prime Minister in a Westminster-type system. It was a singular irony that this visit to see how the committee system worked in Jersey would lead in time to my involvement in bringing that very system to an end. This, though, is the subject of a later account.

I was very pleased when the standing of the Forum was recognised by an invitation which I received from a specialised arm of the OECD to chair a Paris conference on "service quality initiatives". I found the protocol attached to such a meeting rather intriguing. Each of the delegates would have before him or her, lying flat on the table, the relevant national flag, and would raise this to the upright when seeking to intervene in debate. I would then have to say, "I recognise Ireland"!

I resigned as Chairman of the Forum in 1997 because I felt that my knowledge of the government system in Northern Ireland was rapidly getting out of date. Admittedly all four of my successors as Head of the Northern Ireland Civil Service—Sir David Fell, Sir John Semple, Sir Gerry Loughran, and the current incumbent, Sir Nigel Hamilton—have at some time or other worked for me, but I was beginning to recognise how much personalities, programmes and organisations had changed since my retirement. One appreciates and acknowledges the passage of time when approached at some social event by an attractive lady, herself well into middle age, with the greeting "I believe you used to work with my father."

These activities, like most of my working life, had been concerned particularly with Northern Ireland. I was now to be asked to perform on a larger pitch. For some years it had been the practice to invite an outsider to lead a periodic review of the organisation and "top structure" of Whitehall departments; these operations were often referred to as "Wardale Reviews" in recognition of their progenitor. I was, then, honoured, flattered and more than slightly terrified to be asked to lead such a review within the Department of Social Security, an enormous organisation, many times the size of the entire Northern Ireland Civil Service, and accountable for the spending of a formidable percentage of government's total revenue. I would, of course, be supported by aides from the Department itself and the Treasury, but the recommendations would be mine, and mine alone. I would have to conduct a whole series of interviews with the most senior people, from the Permanent Secretary down, and these were to include Nick Montagu (later Chairman of the Board of Inland Revenue), Alice Perkins, the wife of Jack Straw (later Director of the Corporate Development Group at the Cabinet Office), and Michael Bichard (a future Permanent Secretary at the Department of Education).

It was particularly relevant that, in this enormous department, "agentisation" had been extensively introduced. One could see the potential merit of breaking this bureaucratic monolith down into a series of more manageable entities—a departmental "core", with the day to day delivery of its services handled by a series of executive agencies. It did not follow from this departmental devolution that all the new entities would be relatively small and manageable. Indeed, the Benefits Agency alone employed many more than twice the number of personnel in the Northern Ireland Civil Service. One of the most significant agencies was still gearing up to take on its new responsibilities— the Child Support Agency. As I talked to its first Chief Executive, Ros Hepplewhite, enthusiastic and well-organised, I would not foresee the future endless controversy about the effectiveness of these means in obliging parents to support their children.

Given this opportunity to observe at close quarters the operation of the "Next Steps" initiative, I could see both the potential strengths and weaknesses of the agentisation process. A successful agency would have a clear focus, manageable and well understood objectives, and an emphasis on practical service to the public rather than high-fallutin' policy making and daily interaction with ministers. I knew from my own experience how one could be totally caught up in operating the traditional bureaucratic system—drafting Green or White Papers, briefing ministers for cabinet or its committees, marshalling arguments for parliamentary debate or replies to Questions. There was a suspicion that elegant prose could be a better aid to advancement than managerial efficiency. I could not help recalling the hand-over briefing offered me by my predecessor on taking up my first departmental Permanent Secretary post. Dr John Oliver, who sadly died at ninety-two, was a civil servant of great experience and real intellectual distinction, whose spoken arguments matched the superbly legible beauty of his calligraphy. His minutes to ministers or colleagues not only read well, but looked well. In handing the baton of departmental leadership to me, John offered brilliant and witty vignettes of the several personalities principally involved with its varied and challenging functions. Perhaps the most important of these was housing, both because the housing stock still included far too many unfit homes, and because disputes arising out of unfair allocations of public housing had been a major complaint of the "Civil Rights Movement" in Northern Ireland. Describing an individual employed in this field, Dr Oliver had characterised him as "a wonderful person; thoughtful, articulate, hard-working; it's just that somehow, somehow, he never builds any actual houses".

His was a degree of politesse matched in my experience only by Lord Windlesham, one of William Whitelaw's Northern Ireland Office ministers during the first period of "Direct Rule". At that time, new policies within areas previously the concern of the old Northern Ireland government were regularly discussed at a consultative and appointed Advisory Council. On a particular day an unfortunate official so unused to confronting ministers or speaking in public as to be incoherent with nervousness, was expressing to Windlesham and the Advisory Council a series of wholly inaudible opinions. "Mr——," gently observed the Noble Lord, "your observations are so relevant, so extraordinarily interesting, that it would be useful if you spoke a little more loudly." It was such a civilised alternative to "For God's sake, speak up!"

Agencies, then, could represent a new and wholly desirable emphasis on service delivery as distinct from policy making.

What seemed less clear was the precise residual role of the core department, embodying the most senior officials with the easiest and most frequent access to the Secretary of State and his colleagues.

I could see, too, that in time each substantial agency would want to develop its own support services in finance, personnel management, in technological development, and so on. There would, of course, be regular and continuing dialogue between an individual agency and the "core"; but how to ensure adequate contact and coordination as between the agencies themselves? Was there not a danger of reinforcing the "silo mentality", so detrimental to "joined-up government" or, as I have already put it, orchestral playing by all the public instruments?

If this coordination fails, daft things happen both at the highest and lowest levels. Joe Public cannot understand why, just after his main thoroughfare has been resurfaced, it has to be dug up again to supply water mains, natural gas or install communications cabling. Joe Public cannot understand why different arms of the Home Office, responsible on the one hand for immigration controls and on the other for the prison system, could not establish reliable systems of communication which, at the very least, would prevent their own ministers from making fools of themselves in the House of Commons. In an age when a private individual can use his home computer to access zillions of pieces of information, to make travel arrangements, book holidays or hotels, purchase books or other items, it seems absurd that intra-government communications remain so bad. Unhappily, the experience of introducing new computer systems in government has been pretty disastrous.

As a conclusion of my "Wardale Review" of the DSS I made a number of recommendations about organisation and grading. I do not recall that anyone subsequently had the courtesy to tell me which of these had been accepted or rejected, or why.

***

In 1995, it was becoming more and more likely that, at the forthcoming general election, a Labour government would be returned to power. There had been much discussion, in a vague generalised way, of potential constitutional reform: devolution to Scotland or Wales; reform of the House of Lords; greater entrenchment of Human Rights. Amongst well-informed people, however, there was a growing concern that these individual objectives or notions fell far short of offering a coherent integrated plan for the better government of the United Kingdom. Out of this concern there arose the project of a Constitution Unit, independent of politics, which would try to persuade politicians and the wider community that future change should be based on the better understanding of the fundamental issues. The work would be carried forward by a "think tank", headed by Robert Hazell, who had strong bureaucratic and academic credentials, and harnessing the talents of some extremely able younger people.

It was decided to steer this complex exercise through an Advisory Group of great and varied experience. When I was invited to join the group it was made clear to me that the remit would not include the question of devolution in Northern Ireland, a situation regarded as sui generis. I would, instead, bring to the party wide administrative experience of devolution in practice, some of which could be relevant to the issue of Scottish and Welsh devolution. Northern Ireland was, after all, the only part of the United Kingdom with actual experience of operating under devolved powers, and that experience might at worst signpost some minefields to be avoided.

So I agreed to join a most interesting group of people chaired by James Cornford and including Sir William (Kerr) Fraser, a former PUS at the Scottish Office and the able journalist Andrew Marr, first editor of the *Independent* and today a most shrewd analyst of politics for the BBC. As the work of the unit proceeded, we unearthed more and more unanswered questions. What were the implications for Scotland and Wales in terms of participation in Cabinet or the UK Parliament? What about the "West Lothian question"? It seemed inevitable that a Labour government would wish to remove hereditary peers either gradually or over time from the House of Lords. But how would it be composed in the future? And what impact, if any, should a revised basis of composition have on the powers of a House of Lords vis a vis the House of Commons?

My main contribution to the project, whose end product was the publication of a series of well-researched reports, was a paper drawing from Northern Ireland experience some questions which needed to be addressed in the context of devolution. With the encouragement of one of my colleagues, Anthony Wright MP, I used this paper as a basis for an article published in the *Political Quarterly* of April-June 1996 under the title "Devolution—Lessons from Northern Ireland".

It is interesting to recall that, in this article, I queried whether separate Secretaries of State for Northern Ireland, Scotland and Wales could be justified in a stable state of devolution, or whether we should look in the future to a single Secretary of State dealing with these several territories while "maintaining a relatively modest official presence in each devolved jurisdiction".

***

As I have said, my lifelong preference has been to work in and for the public service. From time to time, though, I was asked to take on short-term consultancies in the private sector. All through my working life the letters HMSO (Her Majesty's Stationery Office) had been borne by official publications. However, in the general drive by government to divest itself of responsibilities which could be discharged elsewhere, the Stationery Office had been "floated off" into the private sector.

With the Good Friday Agreement of 1998, there arose the

prospect of a return to devolved government in Northern Ireland, with a potential local Assembly and Executive generating the usual need to publish Reports of Debates, Order Papers, Bills and Acts and various reports or statutory returns. As a consequence, there was potential for substantial business to be won by the Stationery Office or, since there was no compulsion to use them, a credible competitor. In the knowledge that I had great experience of working within a devolved system in Northern Ireland, the Stationery Office chairman invited me to accept appointment as President of the Stationery Office Council for Northern Ireland, and to act in that capacity as consultant and advisor to the Office in its dealings with the recently elected Assembly.

Virtually the first business of that Assembly was to form a sub-group of its members, the Assembly Commission, to consider the practicalities and logistics of getting a deliberative assembly and legislature up and running. Accordingly I sat in with the Stationery Office team when the Commission visited London to discuss the services which the Assembly would need and the Office could provide. Our visitors were impressed by the slick operation which provided with minimal delay the printed Reports of Debates in both Houses of Parliament. It was fascinating, too, to see the huge stock of publications held for issue when appropriate, such as Admiralty Charts.

For me, though, the most striking feature of these conversations was the role of Mr Peter Robinson, then Deputy Leader of the Democratic Unionist Party (DUP). That party had declined to be involved in the negotiations leading to the Good Friday Agreement, and expressed firm opposition to the notion of sharing power in government with a party, Sinn Féin, closely linked to the paramilitary Provisional IRA. It was striking, then, that Robinson, not the warmest of personalities but a person of very considerable executive ability and weight, should show in these exchanges more interest than any other member of the Commission in the fine practical detail of a working Assembly.

***

In 1993 I had been invited to become a member of the Statute Law Advisory Committee for Northern Ireland. This Committee, appointed to advise the Department of Finance, operated in those arcane areas appropriately described as "lawyer's law", and indeed, I believe I was the first (and may have been the last) non-lawyer asked to join that Committee. It was always chaired by a very senior judge—in my earliest days as a member, by Lord Justice Carswell, later to become Lord Chief Justice of Northern Ireland, and today a Lord of Appeal in Ordinary (one of the "Law Lords" who constitute our country's supreme court of final appeal). Other members would be drawn from the Bench, from academic lawyers, and from both branches of the legal profession.

My daughter Caroline, having read Jurisprudence at Oxford, graduated from the Guildford College of Law and taken her articles with the renowned London litigator Herbert Smith, thereupon decided that she did not really like the law at all and preferred to do something totally different. There were, I confess, times on the Statute Law Advisory Committee when I had some sympathy with her decision. Ironically, Herbert Smith acted for Arthur Andersen in the prolonged law suit arising out of the De Lorean debacle and the allegedly negligent performance of its audit responsibility, and I found myself giving evidence, under rigorous cross-examination by tough American lawyers, which was filmed and could potentially be used as evidence at the trial in America. While this ordeal was in progress, Caroline was working away on some other issue umpteen floors above me.

My own limited knowledge of the law, in academic terms, arose out of the inclusion in the Modern History course at Oxford of some study of constitutional law (I still remember "The King and De Keyser's Royal Hotel"). Of course as a civil servant I had been obliged to apply myself to many relevant statutes, and had even been in at the birth of some of them, in helping to form instructions to the draftsman.

People often complained about the impenetrable prolixity of much statute law. There was a legend that an earlier experience of trying to draft in the plainest of simple English had left so many loose ends as to provoke innumerable law suits and an ultimate change in the law itself. A very distinguished Ulsterman, Sir Patrick Macrory, who had been employed briefly as a very young man in the office of Parliamentary Counsel in London, would sometimes claim with pride that he had drafted the only section of the immensely complex post-war Town and Country Planning Act that had not given rise to any subsequent litigation. "And what did that section say, Patrick?" "This Act shall not apply to Northern Ireland."

I had enjoyed two wonderful parodies of the draftsman's art, in each case dealing with that important Section of a typical Act which seeks to give a clear definition of terms used elsewhere. In one case "bookmaker" is defined (rather neatly, I think) as "the person to whom the person making the bet looks for the payment of his winnings, if any". In the other "greyhound racing" is defined as "a sport in which a greyhound is encouraged to move in a forwards direction by means of a simulacrum of its natural quarry, mechanically propelled before it".

For much of my life, even if not fully able to understand, I have been able and willing to chance my arm. I have managed to serve on several Audit Committees, and indeed to chair a couple of them, without revealing to the full my essentially innumerate nature. I confess without shame that I did not always fully understand what my fellow members of the Statute Law Advisory Committee were talking about. Yet the issues, albeit academic and even mysterious in form, could have real practical importance. To what extent, for example, should persons living together over a long period without the bond of marriage enjoy rights comparable with those of partners in conventional relationships? How did one strike the balance between the responsibility of a property owner to keep passage over his land as safe as possible with the expectation on a user to behave sensibly? It was an intellectual treat to hear such issues knowledgeably debated by expert professionals, but this was a (happily) rare case in which I felt that my contribution, while well intentioned, had been of limited value.

***

However, I was not deterred by my experience on the Law Reform Advisory Committee from responding in 2003 to an advertisement seeking applications for the Chairmanship of a new statutory body, the Legal Services Commission for Northern Ireland.

For many years the responsibility for dealing with applications for Legal Aid had rested with the Legal Aid Committee of the Incorporated Law Society of Northern Ireland. While there was no reason to doubt that the members of that Committee had approached their responsibilities conscientiously and without bias, the "optics" of decisions by a committee of lawyers affecting the remuneration of their own profession were not favourable. In the case of criminal Legal Aid, the decision to grant or withhold rested with the court, and the responsibility of the staff of the Legal Aid Department had been simply to vet the resultant claims and disburse the monies due to solicitors and members of the Bar. In the case of civil Legal Aid, however, there were decisions to be taken about means and eligibility. Clearly there were major challenges arising in this whole area, both at the local and national levels. In Northern Ireland there were some horrendous backlogs in processing claims, while the Lord Chancellor's department was seriously concerned about the inexorable rise in the costs of the system, particularly on the criminal side.

I was interviewed by senior officials of the Courts Service, the Lord Chancellor's "arm" in Northern Ireland, and offered what promised to be a most interesting and challenging post. For some months, before the formal handover from the Law Society, we operated in shadow, allowing time for induction and for familiarisation with extensive preparatory work already carried out for the Courts Service by Deloitte consultants. I made a point of asking for, and carefully scanning, a representative selection of case files. I was astonished by the complexity of certain types of case, particularly where medical or other negligence was alleged. Here the taxpayer could find himself paying for the services not only of solicitors and counsel (often both Senior and Junior) but of a whole range of expert witnesses. I was struck also by the fact that solicitors carefully recorded the hours of work devoted to a legally-aided case, but there seemed to be no satisfactory way of judging whether the time spent was necessary or excessive. I have always found it interesting and useful to "read across" from one area of experience to another, and I recalled from some work in the field of NHS dentistry that the Dental Practice Review Board was in a position to monitor treatment patterns and question unexplained deviations from the norm.

On the face of it, our priorities were to iron out inefficiencies in the system, reduce and ideally eliminate backlogs, and make proposals to relate the availability of civil Legal Aid to clearly demonstrable social need. It was this apparent task of research leading to reform which had attracted to the Commission a body of members of formidable weight and experience. However, early discussions with Lord Filkin, at that time the responsible minister at the Lord Chancellor's Department, made it clear that a major objective was to bring the escalating costs of the scheme under control.

I had an opportunity to provide a foundation manifesto when asked to speak at a conference on "Legal Aid Tomorrow", held at the Waterfront Hall in Belfast on 13 November 2003 before a large audience of practitioners. I was able to report that I had already met the Lord Chief Justice, other members of the judiciary, representatives of the solicitor's profession and the Bar, and organisations such as the Housing Rights Service and the Citizens Advice Bureau. I spoke of the need for change, but emphasised that we would seek to base it upon empirical evidence, and wherever possible, expose our provisional views to comment and criticism. I said our aim would be to develop a Northern Ireland service to meet Northern Ireland conditions, although we had to be conscious that what we proposed must seem fair, just and equitable, not only to members from Northern Ireland constituencies, but to that great majority of parliamentarians who represented other areas of the United Kingdom. Our aim, as I put it, must be "to marshal together in a grand alliance all who have a contribution to make in providing to those who most need it the best possible means to identify and secure their rights". I announced our determination to launch ourselves upon a painstaking and comprehensive programme of research, some of it conducted "in-house" and otherwise undertaken by academic or other professionals. We needed to identify the real "cost drivers" and to begin setting a logical order of priorities; to prepare for the ultimate separation of criminal aid and civil aid into separate funds.

Because I was fortunate enough to have such talented colleagues, and there was so much to do, I decided to set up an extensive series of committees to ensure that every member had a deeper involvement and commitment than a monthly attendance at a full Commission meeting. I was particularly happy that Jeremy Harbison, an analytical thinker of the first order, agreed to head up our research committee.

Unhappily two time-bombs, one collective and the other personal, were ticking away. Acting on advice from consultants, the "old" Legal Aid Committee had decided to authorise a substantial increase in the standard rates for various types of work by solicitors. It was true that these standard rates had remained unaltered for a considerable time; yet the total funds disbursed under the scheme had increased steadily as many cases were identified as "exceptional" and meriting higher remuneration. The head of the Northern Ireland Court Service, feeling that the Service had not been adequately consulted, and dubious of the Treasury's willingness to fund the increased costs, had used his authority as an Accounting Officer to instruct the Chief Executive of the Legal Aid Department not to make payments at the enhanced level. His Committee, in spite of this, instructed him to do so. Placed in what one could only recognise as a most unenviable position, he responded to the instructions of his employers rather than their paymasters "across the road".

When the Commission took over, we too urgently sought the best available legal advice and concluded that, as a public body, we must defer to the instructions of the relevant Accounting Officer. Thus, instead of forging a friendly and constructive partnership with the profession, as we would have wished, we were put into the invidious position of being demonised by it. Our Chief Executive, Gerry Crossan, received in consequence some unforgivably personal and offensive letters, which did not sit well with the profession's high esteem for itself. On the other hand, solicitors' practices were small businesses and needed some certainty about a large part of their income. It soon became clear that the whole matter could only be resolved through Judicial Review. How could one reconcile the powers and responsibilities of an Accounting Officer under Treasury rules with a statutory obligation to pay "fair and reasonable remuneration"?

Unhappily, just as it became clear that leadership of the Commission would make great demands upon the time and energy of the incumbent, the growing pressures aggravated a chronic chest condition that left me immobilised for days at a time. When Lord Filkin returned to Belfast for a further meeting, I had no alternative but to tell him that I felt unable to continue as chairman in what was proving close to a full-time job. I had served, in shadow or in office, for less than a year, and I had never before, since entering the Civil Service more than fifty years ago, been obliged to leave a job barely begun. My successor was to be Sir Anthony Holland, already chairman of the Northern Ireland Parades Commission. Had he been born Japanese, I am sure he would have made an ideal kamikaze pilot!

**

In writing earlier of the book of essays produced by the Chief Executives Forum, I have described how and why it came about that I spent some little time in Jersey, exploring its system of committee-based government. In my essay, "A View from Jersey", I had acknowledged some great differences between the two jurisdictions in the following terms:

> There are, of course, great differences between Jersey and Northern Ireland: differences of scale, of the degree of operating autonomy, and of political culture. In the case of the island, we have a government with an annual budget of around £300 million a year expended for the benefit of a population of around 85,000; we have a jurisdiction not subject within its own competence to the ultimate authority of Her Majesty's government or of the UK Parliament; we have a culture in which candidates stand for election to the States as individuals, rather than as the standard bearers for a political party... The greatest contrast between the two jurisdictions, however, is that whereas in Jersey all the locally elected politicians are directly involved in the executive government of the island, as well as in making its laws, in Northern Ireland none of the locally elected politicians is currently so involved.

When I wrote this after my brief visit in 1997 I was not aware that concern was mounting within Jersey itself, despite its attachment to distinctive and traditional ways, that the prevailing system of government there was ill-suited to meet the growing challenges of the modern world. There was a rising tide of opinion amongst both politicians and the public that the time had come for a searching and independent reappraisal of the system of government. Understandably those concerned felt that such an appraisal could best be carried out by bringing distinguished Jersey residents not involved in active politics together with experts from the United Kingdom familiar with systems and problems of government. I doubt if my name would have emerged as a potential member without my relatively recent contact with Colin Powell, who had just retired as Chief Adviser to the States and would serve on the body himself as one of the domestic "team". At any rate I was sounded about my availability and willingness to serve, and since I have had a long-running interest in the organisation of government, I was most happy to accept.

On 2 March 1999, then, the island's ancient legislature, the States of Jersey, resolved to appoint a Review Panel to make recommendations as to how the existing machinery of government could be improved. The group would be chaired by Sir Cecil ("Spike") Clothier QC, a distinguished lawyer, and a former Parliamentary Commissioner for Administration, or "Ombudsman", who had been earlier involved in a review of Jersey's unique policing arrangements, and had served in the UK as chairman of an impressive range of commissions and enquiries. Although already eighty years of age and not in the best of health, his intellect remained as sharp as a needle, and he was to prove wonderful company. Another appointee from the mainland would be Sir Maurice Shock, a former Vice-Chancellor of Leicester University and Rector of Lincoln College, Oxford (as it happens, Clothier's old college). While Fellow and Praelector in Politics at University College he had tutored (amongst many others) a certain William Jefferson Clinton, an American Rhodes Scholar.

Some years later I would attend a "Tip O'Neill Lecture" at the Derry campus of the University of Ulster given by Senator Hillary Clinton. She was not accompanied to the lecture by her husband Bill, who was signing copies of his recently-published autobiography in Belfast. However, as we sat down to dinner after the lecture, I noticed a vacant seat a couple of places to the left of me, and well into the meal the ex-President arrived, was introduced to everyone, and occupied this empty chair. I had met Clinton during his presidency, in the limited sense of shaking his hand in Belfast, but it seemed crass to refer to this. However, at the end of the meal I could not resist approaching the great man to ask, "Does the name Maurice Shock mean anything to you?" For a dreadful moment I feared he might reply, "Maurice who?" Instead his face lit up with his incomparable charm and he said, "My God, Maurice taught me politics!" "Well," I thought, "he seems to have taught you pretty effectively."

The third member of our UK quartet was Professor Michael Clarke of the University of Birmingham, a recognised academic expert on the workings of English local government. As the fourth extra-insular member it was a real honour and pleasure to serve alongside people of such experience and distinction.

The native Jersey component included Colin Powell, for so many years a key figure in the local administration, a couple of acute local lawyers, a media expert and the delightful Mrs Anne Perchard, a recognised world authority on the celebrated Jersey cattle, who would on occasions generously load the deprived colleagues from across the water with Jersey Royal new potatoes from her own farm. George MacRae was a wonderful secretary to the panel.

We would normally meet in the building in the centre of St Helier occupied by the legislature and Royal Court, take lunch together at the delightfully old-fashioned Victoria Club, before returning (in the case of Clothier, Shock and myself) to the civilised retreat of the Hotel l'Horizon on St Brelade's Bay. I recall in particular one warm summer evening when we decided to order up a room-service dinner and consume it on the balcony of Spike's room, looking out across the glorious sandy beach to the sea. Just as the waiter arrived with our food, Maurice decided that he should first use what Americans decorously term "the facilities". At the very moment after he disappeared through the door into Spike's suite, the largest seagull in Jersey—indeed almost a mini-albatross—evoked the days of German occupation of Jersey by dive-bombing like a Stuka and, with great speed and dexterity, carrying off the Shock dinner into the air. I can still see the look of surprise and dismay on the face of Sir Maurice Shock as he returned to confront an empty plate. Shock tactics indeed!

Of course much of our time was devoted to considering written and oral evidence from Jersey politicians, officials and other interests. At times Clothier's earlier judicial experience as a Recorder proved particularly useful, as when a political figure from outside the island, who had better remain nameless in his own interest, seemed to think that he was there to take evidence from us rather than we from him. Spike courteously but very firmly explained to him that this was not the case.

It goes without saying that our witnesses included not only the current Bailiff, Sir Philip Bailhache, but predecessors in that office of First Citizen of the Island. I was taken by surprise at an early evidence session when Sir Peter Crill, Bailhache's immediate predecessor, pointed a finger at me before even sitting down, and said, "We had the same headmaster, you know." At first I was quite mystified by this comment, until I recalled that John Grummitt, Principal of the Royal Belfast Academical Institution when I attended it in the Forties, had come to us from Victoria College, Jersey in time to avoid the German Occupation. Nor was this Crill's only surprising Ulster connection, for he had married a Miss Dodd from Dromara, County Down, who had studied medicine at Queen's alongside the wife of a close friend of mine. Later the Crills would graciously entertain us in their beautiful home, one of Jersey's "cod houses" built in the days when cod fishing on the Grand Banks had been one of the props of the insular economy (nowadays heavily dependent on off-shore finance and tax benefits).

I grew to understand over time in how many ways Jersey was a unique place. Isolated and singularly beautiful both along its magnificent coastline and in its miniature inland landscapes, it also retained fascinating residues of its Anglo-Norman heritage. Although the local patois had largely disappeared from current use, many of the islanders still carried French names, and when we attended the States and the names of members were called out, non-attendants would be registered by a cry of "absent de l'isle". A Governor would occupy a throne as representative of the Crown, while the Bailiff would preside as Speaker, a role improbably combined with that of Chief Justice; and although not directly involved in the executive business of government, he would tend to front up any delegation to Westminster or encounter with a British Minister visiting the island. There was the further singularity that three types of member sat together in the States, with the same legislative and executive roles, albeit returned to serve there by different routes: "connétables" or constables because chosen by a Parish to head its local administration; "députés" or deputies elected from a constituency based on a local area; and "senateurs" or senators elected on an all-island franchise. The Parish remained a vital element in Jerseyan life, and indeed in earlier days the Parish Clergy themselves had been members of the States.

I learned for the first time that, although permanent settlement in Jersey by an outsider required considerable assets (as evidenced by residents like Graham Hill or Alan Whicker), much of the donkey-work on the island's farms, hotels, bars and restaurants was being performed by Portuguese nationals, many of them from Madeira. One was much more likely to hear Portuguese in Jersey than French or a local version of it.

Because Jersey had originally been a possession of the Dukes of Normandy, it first became associated with the British Crown with the Norman Conquest and the accession of William I to the crown of England. However, Jersey (and its sister jurisdiction of Guernsey) decided to retain the link with the Crown after

England lost its continental foothold. From this history there flowed, amongst other features of the island life, a distinctive legal code and system differing from the English norm.

I was intrigued to note how separate from each other Jersey and Guernsey remained, although we did have one joint meeting at St Helier airport with a Guernsey group covering ground rather similar to our own enquiry. My sole visit to Guernsey itself came about by climatic accident. I had long been intrigued by the survival on Sark, albeit part of the Guernsey bailiwick, of elements of feudal overlordship. During and after the Second World War, the Seigneurie had been occupied by the famous Dame of Sark, Dame Sybil Hathaway, who had treated the occupying force with aristocratic hauteur, and had put the garrison to work on tasks of public utility as soon as the capitulation had been announced.

I had therefore taken time out to make the ferry journey from Jersey for an overnight stay on Sark at the delightful Stocks Hotel, an ideal place for anyone wishing to complete a thesis or write a book in absolute tranquillity. With no vehicular traffic, I was able to traverse the tiny island on foot, and to visit in particular the sumptuous gardens of the Seigneurie, now occupied by the reigning Seigneur, Michael Beaumont, a grandson of the celebrated Dame. An idyllic day was rounded off by a wonderful dinner in the tranquil oasis of my hotel.

Unfortunately the weather changed severely overnight, and I woke to find scuds of rain driven by winds of near gale-force. To my dismay, the proprietress told me at breakfast that ferry services to Jersey had been suspended for the day; embarrassing news, since I was due to fly from St Helier back to Belfast that very evening. "But if you run," she suggested helpfully, "you might just catch the ferry to Guernsey, which is much closer and may well be the last of the day." So I took my little overnight case and ran—no taxis on Sark!—down to the tiny harbour and caught the ferry in the nick of time. The relatively short passage to St Peter Port which followed was tempestuous, and not a few of my fellow passengers gave a convincing demonstration of serious vomiting. From the harbour at St Peter Port I took a taxi to Guernsey's airport, and was lucky to be able to buy a seat on the short hop to Jersey in a plane so tiny that we were individually weighed before boarding and given seats carefully chosen to balance the flimsy aircraft. I had the impression of a flight so short that fastening my seat-belt and unfastening it seemed close to a single movement. Altogether it was quite an adventure, but I would love to return one day to Sark, in spite of the progressive erosion of its distinctively feudal system of government.

Of course the main focus of our Panel's inquiry was upon that very "committee system" which I had studied for quite different reasons some time before. All the major functions of government (and some quite minor ones) were entrusted to separate Committees of the States. The Policy and Resources Committee, chaired at that time by the far-sighted Senator Pierre Horsfall, had some influence on the coordination of policy and executive action, but its chairman was far from being the equivalent of a Prime, First or Chief Minister. In earlier times the Isle of Man, another Crown dependency not a part of the United Kingdom, had operated on a similar basis, but had since moved to a ministerial system with what seemed to be beneficial results. We travelled as a Panel to the Isle of Man to meet leading figures there, and it was odd to recall that my only previous visit to a place so close to Northern Ireland had been as a small boy on holiday before the Second World War.

As we took and studied our evidence, we became more and more persuaded that the committee system was not "fit for purpose" in the modern world. We found it to be confused, procrastinatory, and lacking in coherence. In some sense all members of the States were "in government" or at least in part of it; what, then, of the role of legislators in holding their government to account? The main thrust of the Clothier Report, when we published it in December 2000, was an argument for collective ministerial government, and a clear distinction between those who governed and those who held them accountable.

It also seemed rather absurd to have three categories of members sitting in the same States assembly, and in particular we did not see why the election of a Constable as the person most suitable to oversee Parish administration should necessarily qualify him to participate in the assembly of the whole island. We were also uncomfortable that a single officer, the Bailiff, should at one and the same time be the nominal head of the executive branch, speaker of the legislature and chief justice.

The publication of our report produced startling headlines in the *Jersey Evening Post*, and we were well aware from the outset of the deep attachment of Jersey men and women to their traditional institutions and procedures, some of them as wholesome as they were unique. It soon became clear that local people were comfortable with the role of the Bailiff as it stood, although I myself continue to feel that it is anomalous at a time when the Lord Chancellor retreats to become a Secretary of State for Justice while the Lords are taking the responsibility for electing their own Speaker. Nor was it wholly a surprise that popular opinion preferred to keep the Constables in the States assembly. In many ways the Parish remains the centre of Jersey life.

As for our central proposition—a move to ministerial government—there was initial concern that an inevitable outcome would be the evolution of a party system to replace the present election of States members on their individual merits. Should it not be right for each States member to be free to state and vote according to his opinion on any matter?

Against this background, Senator Horsfall decided to invite me back to Jersey to address a well-attended meeting of States members on the benefits of collective responsibility. In my native Northern Ireland, the old "Stormont" governments, admittedly party-based, had adhered strictly to the principle of collective responsibility, and indeed, I recalled the dismissal in the Fifties of an Attorney General who was deemed to have breeched it. The failure to accept collective responsibility had, I believed, been one of the greatest weaknesses in the new model for Northern Ireland government established under the Good Friday Agreement, and this was to be amply demonstrated when an individual minister was able to make a major policy pronouncement without the approval of his Executive colleagues or any evidence that the elected Assembly would be willing to implement it.

In true Jersey fashion, action in response to the Clothier Report was taken only after prolonged controversy, deliberation and debate. However, I can now reflect on what a pleasure and privilege it had been to work with distinguished colleagues, to come to know a most fascinating jurisdiction under the Crown, and to play a part in a fundamental change which will, I hope, serve Jersey well in the future. Today, Senator Frank Walker presides over a Council of Ministers as Chief Minister of the Island, and I wish him, his nine ministerial colleagues, and his fellow-islanders every happiness and success.

Since, in finalising our report, I had majored on the questions of accountability and scrutiny of executive action, it was a great satisfaction to read in a published guide to ministerial government in Jersey an emphasis on creating not a politically adversarial system but a means of ensuring "well-informed, constructive but sometimes critical comment about existing and proposed policies and legislation". I was happy to see in these words a reflection of the final paragraph of our report (which I had drafted). "We believe", it read, "that Jersey... could become a shining example of a true modern democracy... That special responsibility we recommend for a Council of Ministers can and should be exercised in a true partnership with the people of Jersey and those they chose to represent them."

The ministerial system, still so new, now faces a severe test in reacting to the scandals of Haut de Garenne. It must now prove itself to be open, accountable and decisive.

[46]

***

If involvement in the affairs of Jersey was a welcome challenge away from home, another commission would take me much further afield.

One day at Belfast International Airport, I had encountered an old Civil Service colleague, David Clement, who since retirement had become involved with an ambitious and growing consultancy, the Helm Corporation, based in the small local town of Moira. The consultancy, David told me, had become particularly active in Bangladesh where, with support from the British Department for International Development (DfID), it had established a Financial Management Academy to build up the expertise of rising members of the Bangladeshi Civil Service. As luck would have it, David had with him that day Helm's project leader in Bangladesh, and there and then they asked me if I would be interested in spending a month or so in the capital, Dacca, to lecture to a course of promising younger officials.

I confess that my knowledge of Bangladesh at that time was not extensive. I associated it in my mind, for the most part, with emigration, poverty, flooding, famine and disaster. I knew, of course, that it had been part of Bengal under the British Raj, and subsequently East Pakistan, before breaking away into independence with Indian support. I remembered the probably apocryphal story that, prior to the final British withdrawal from the sub-continent, the post-war Labour government had chosen to appoint as the last Governor of Bengal a worthy who had entered politics as an active member of the railwaymens' trade union. "Ah," someone had said at the Carlton Club. "Up to now they've been chosen for their prowess at huntin' and shootin'. Now we will have someone better at shuntin' and hootin'."

Apart from a very brief visit to Bombay and Delhi, I had no experience of the subcontinent when I arrived in Dacca in the spring of 1998. That huge Asian city was a culture shock of the first order; some fourteen million people huddled together in an enormous human ant-heap, with livestock at the roadside, crude cricket on any level waste ground, endless bicycle rickshaws and the most beat-up buses on the planet. They, like the trains, had passengers sitting on roofs, hanging out of windows or securing any hand-hold available. I was ferried through pulsating streets to the project's residence in one of the more respectable areas of the city, and relieved to realise that there was air conditioning and a curious type of slow-burning candle to discourage the mosquitoes.

My lectures were to be given in an office building in the city centre to a group of thirty or so agreeable, curious and sometimes obstreperous young men, including the then Private Secretary to the Finance Minister. I would take a packed lunch with me, and enjoyed my work there, except on one occasion when a power failure—apparently a frequent occurrence in the city—stalled an overcrowded lift between floors. Like everywhere else in Dacca the press of humanity was all too evident, and I had visions of sharing the company of half the population of Dacca for hours on end when happily the power was restored and we returned to earth.

I may say that I am beginning to have a phobia about lifts. On a later occasion Elizabeth and I were guests at a Graduation Ceremony of the Open University, an institution I greatly admire, held at the Whitla Hall of Queen's University in Belfast. The post-graduation reception was to be held across the road in the Staff Common Room, and we joined in a lift there Lady Daniel, the wife of the then Open University Vice Chancellor, together with the Honorary Graduate of the day and his elderly mother. When this lift, too, became stuck between floors, it took a strikingly long time for anyone to wonder why we had not turned up, and I am not sure that the dignity of the occasion was much enhanced when we had to be rescued by members of the fire brigade.

Because I knew so little about Bangladesh and its Civil Service, I had taken the precaution before leaving of searching the internet for any relevant background, and was fortunate enough to unearth a learned and informative article by a professor at the University of Dacca. When this aroused great interest on the part of one of the local officials organising the course, it struck me that it was probably easier for me to access such information in Belfast via the web than to go looking for it at the university round the corner.

Inevitably I experienced some encounters with the expatriate community. A well-appointed British Club, impressively guarded and protected, offered the weekend luxury of a swimming pool and pints of cold beer. I was also entertained at the ultra-modern residence of the British High Commissioner, at a reception given for visitors from the oil industry.

I will always remember from that extraordinary month two sorties out of Dacca. With some of the permanent members of the project team, we took a picnic visit to Comilla, right on the frontier with India; clearly not one of the world's flashpoint frontiers, because there was no formal frontier post and we were able to photograph each other one foot into India and one foot back into Bangladesh. Back on the "right" side, a friendly local police officer suggested we eat our lunch in his ramshackle hut, piled to the ceiling with aging files dating back to the days of the Raj, and, for all I know, to Queen Victoria herself. At nearby Maynamati we stopped to look at some ancient ruins, but also to visit the moving and meticulously maintained Commonwealth War Graves cemetery with its white headstones all the more striking amongst beautiful tropical shrubs and the colourful saris of local women.

One of the Bangladeshi course organisers suggested that we should visit the Parliament Building, a remarkable piece of ultra-modern architecture with moat-like water features. There, a delightful little lady conducted me with pride around the Parliamentary Library—volume after volume of statutes and debates under successive British, Pakistani and Bangladeshi sovereignty. We paused respectfully before a much-thumbed edition of Erskine May. "That," said this devout Muslim lady, "is our bible, you know." My escort then took me to see the Clerk of Parliament, a friend of his, who surprisingly said, "I think the Speaker would be interested to meet you. Could you come back another day?" So it was that I came to meet the very urbane Honourable Humayun Rasheed Choudhury MP, who presented me with a heavy gold (in colour) medallion which sits today in my trophy cabinet at home.

At first his main theme was the desirability of achieving for their current President a Nobel Peace Prize. He himself had previously served as Foreign Minister and for a term as President of the General Assembly of the United Nations. Did I realise, he asked, how important it was that a long-running insurgency in part of their country was now being brought to a peaceful end; weapons were being handed over and former dissidents garlanded with flowers? So it was that conditions in the Chittagong Hill Tracts, mostly occupied by "tribals" rather than Muslim Bengalis, were returning to normal after many years.

This was the very moment at which peace processes and prospective decommissioning of weaponry were at the top of the Northern Ireland agenda, and so I expressed great interest in what he had just told me. To my astonishment he then said, "If you are interested, we could arrange to take you in there."

Accordingly, a couple of days later, I found myself sitting in the VIP lounge of Dacca Airport with a "minder" who would accompany me. At first we were alone, but after a short time we were joined by a local MP about to fly to some other destination, and clad in the garb of an ultra-orthodox Muslim. My companion chatted amicably enough to him until he departed, and then hissed, "He is a fanatic!"

We took our Biman Airways flight to Chittagong, and from there travelled by car deep into an area strikingly different from the dead-level countryside of mainstream Bangladesh, with its elevated main roads to keep traffic as far as possible above the regular flood-water. The Hill Tracts are beautiful areas of upland:

great stands of teak, rubber plantations, tea gardens. My base was to be the Circuit House at Kagrachari, which embodied the office of the local District Commissioner and accommodation for visiting ministers, senior officials or judges. I was welcomed and hospitably entertained, although breakfast, lunch and dinner all seemed to consist of the same ingredients, and I wondered about the alleged pacification when I found an armed soldier of the Bangladesh Rifles guarding my bedroom. As dawn broke, I could hear the muezzin intoning the call to prayer from a mosque in the town below. The next day I had a pretty comprehensive tour, meeting "tribals" in colourful and distinctive costumes, and finding my guardians of the Bangladesh Rifles still bearing the unmistakeable marks of British military tradition. At dinner later in the guest house I met one of the leaders of the Shanti Bahini (the local Provos, as it were) and learned something of the assurances and compromises which had led to the formal abandonment of their struggle.

On the way back to Chittagong next day, I realised we had just passed a local school. "Do you think I could make a short visit?" I asked. We turned round at once, and I paid a visit that was wholly unexpected and for which there could clearly have been no preparation. I was enormously impressed by the neatness, cleanliness and good behaviour of children in this remote backwater. Bangladesh may not have been a perfect democracy, but in any country it is an encouraging sign of freedom and openness when a foreign visitor is allowed to see for himself on the basis of a spontaneous suggestion.

The visit was to conclude, before my return to Dacca, with a lunch given by the Divisional Commissioner, whose word, as far as I could see, was law for about twenty million people. His residence was large and his company and hospitality agreeable, but I was keenly aware of a commitment to speak that evening at the British Council in Dacca to local newspaper editors. As the leisurely lunch proceeded, I became more and more conscious of a worrying approach towards the scheduled departure time for my flight back to the capital. "Do not be concerned," said the Commissioner, sensing my anxiety. "We will get you there." Perilously close to check-in time the Commissioner and I boarded a formidable vehicle accompanied by a heavily-armed bodyguard. As we reached the main road to Chittagong Airport, I could see utter gridlock ahead of us in the form of innumerable heavy lorries. I shrugged my shoulders in despair. "Do not be concerned," repeated the Commissioner. At that the armed bodyguard left our car, pointed his weapon in the air, made urgent and decisive gestures and—lo and behold—like the fabled parting of the Red Sea, the lorries pulled over to the perilous boundaries of the adjoining ditches, and we sailed serenely through. Thus it was that we arrived a mere fifteen minutes after departure time. In the meantime, however, the Commissioner had sent a telephone message for the plane to be held until I arrived. Yet even his authority fell a little short when we drove to the very steps of the aircraft and the Commissioner attempted to have me admitted without a boarding card. Even in ignorance of Bengali, it was possible to get the broad drift that nobody short of the President of the People's Republic of Bangladesh would be allowed to board a scheduled flight without a boarding card. I entered the terminal, was briskly processed, bade farewell to the Commissioner with a degree of relief, and took my place amongst the sweating, and probably resentful, local passengers.

Back in the capital, the venue of the British Council enabled me to take in a wonderful travelling exhibition about Britain's historic links with the Muslim world, a true knowledge of which should give each party cause to reflect. Thereafter I spoke to a group of editors about the work of the BBC, and found that, whatever the views of the listeners, viewers and licence payers at home, the World Service was regarded as a far more honest and reliable source of information about world and local events than any other. Yet I suspect they found the concept of a national broadcaster free from government control hard to grasp or even unbelievable. When one editor said, "Of course, we were so grateful for your support during our War of Independence," I had to remind him that the BBC did not take sides inside or outside our own country, but simply tried to present the objective truth to the best of its ability. If that truth was helpful, so be it.

As my visit came to an end, I reflected on what I had learned about government in this country of some 120 million people at that time. I had met the Speaker, been entertained by the Comptroller and Auditor General and a group of Permanent Secretaries, who generously gave me a very beautiful hand-embroidered coverlet, and enjoyed regular dialogue with my likeable group of students. Their generation were keen for reform, but complained that too many ministers felt they had accomplished all that was required in obtaining a government office and car. I had been a little depressed by an exchange with quite a senior official. "Where do you serve?" I asked. "In the Ministry of Finance." "Oh, that is a very good place to be in any administration." "No, Sir. Very few opportunities for foreign travel." It did not seem encouraging if posts in government were downgraded because they involved service in and for the country. The future lay with people like my temporary students, and I was greatly pleased when the University of Ulster made an arrangement to further the studies and deepen the knowledge of this group and their successors.

I had enjoyed and been fascinated by my visit to Bangladesh, but in the nature of things never expected to return. However, the Helm Corporation continued to be deeply and constructively involved there. In mid-2007 John Wallace, their principal representative in Dacca, called to see me during a visit home. At our meeting he explained to me that the consultancy were heavily involved in a project to buttress the skills of the most senior officers in the Bangladesh government. Would I come out once again to Dacca in early November to take part in a seminar for the Secretaries of their government departments? While the thought of so long a journey and the accompanying health measures gave me a moment's pause, I found it a challenge too interesting to reject. It occurred to me that I could travel by Emirates, break the journey in Dubai, and spend a little time there with Elizabeth before flying on to Bangladesh. So it was that we spent a few days together on the Gulf, and visited opulent hotels, magnificent golf courses and huge shopping malls. Contacts there generously entertained us in superb restaurants. The sea was warm and a brilliant blue. We were glad to have seen it, but would not be avid to return. It is the most extravagantly opulent of places with its man-made islands and other mind-blowing features. Too much, for our taste, like a resplendent Disneyland. Native Emiratis are few and far between. Alongside the aloof Arabs and the high-spending visitors, including growing numbers of newly rich from Russia, are the true work-horses of Dubai, legions of Indians, Pakistanis or Bangladeshis toiling on construction sites under the blazing sun, or driving one of the multitude of taxis—for there is no effective public transport—to support a wife and family back in the Indian sub-continent and rarely seen. Work on ever more megalomaniac projects proceeds apace. Florence is to be reproduced in the desert. Meanwhile cranes rise everywhere over the world's largest building site.

On 2 November Elizabeth left for home while I resumed the journey to Dacca. It was an interesting time to return to Bangladesh. It is one of those countries in which, from time to time, corruption becomes so endemic that the military decide to throw the rascals out and start again. Now the two women who have dominated local politics have been pushed aside and the senior person in an interim government is not a Prime Minister but a "chief adviser". I spent two whole days in conclave with very senior officials, one of them the cabinet secretary and another the chief adviser to the chief adviser, a graduate of the Harvard Business School and a pretty tough cookie. Sessions would begin with a reading from the Koran. I had some opportunity to tour the city, as crowded as ever with innumerable bicycle rickshaws, and with all the signs of extensive poverty. It is a society in which middle-ranking officials are very poorly paid, and there is an understandable temptation to grant favours to fellow-citizens offering a few takka. On my final day I was taken out of the city by John Wallace to see some grass-root efforts to promote self-sufficiency. Unexpectedly I was asked to speak at a crowded outdoor village gathering, with each sentence translated into Bengali to gratifying applause, and thereafter, to hand over gifts of little goats to half a dozen village women, and to be photographed beside the new fish-pond holding a net full of wriggling monsters. Once again it was a fascinating and chastening experience, and I returned with the generous gift of a magnificent quilt beautifully embroidered with birds, beasts and flowers.

2

The Health of the Nation

WHEN I WORKED IN THE UNITED States in the early Sixties, as Deputy Director of the British Industrial Development Office in New York, I would often find myself enjoying a meal with executives from some American company in Chicago or Detroit or Los Angeles. I was struck by how often, after we had exhausted the main business of possible direct investment in the United Kingdom, I would be quizzed about our National Health Service. From these exchanges, I surmised that the powerful medical lobby in the USA had done a pretty good job of convincing "middle America" that "socialised medicine" would be a first step down a slippery slope towards the displacement of Henry Ford by Karl Marx.

Yet I had grown up with the NHS as a powerful and desirable fact of national life. Introduced when I was still in my mid-teens, I had been grateful for its services on occasions when I had needed general practitioner, dental or hospital treatment. I can recall how horrified I was when an American employee at our New York office told me of the cost of some dental reconstruction for which she had paid. Hopefully she had been able to draw upon private insurance, but this itself would have been far from cheap. Americans, I had noticed, set great store on perfect dentition as a cardinal feature of their appearance and personal presentation. People presenting a dingy oral image were too easily recognised as European, and probably English, visitors. Much later I would sit at a dinner table in Belfast with Congressman Robert Kennedy Jr, and been as much struck by his glittering dentition as by his tendentious and ill-informed views about Northern Ireland. He slightly redeemed himself for the latter by sending me a sympathetic letter when the Provisional IRA disobligingly blew up our house around us; but, as I observed in my reply, he came from a family better placed than most to appreciate the consequences of violent fanaticism.

By 1992, Brian Mawhinney, the Member of Parliament for Peterborough and a former Junior Minister at the Northern Ireland Office, had become Minister of State at the Department of Health in Whitehall, then led by Virginia Bottomley as Secretary of State. At that time, neither the Conservative nor the Labour Party fought elections in Northern Ireland, and thus an Ulsterman could become a member of a British government only by winning a seat in Great Britain. This, Mawhinney—like myself an old boy of the Royal Belfast Academical Institution—had done. Many of my colleagues in the Northern Ireland Civil Service had found him abrasive, but for whatever reason he and I had got on well with each other.

Amongst the many problems confronting Virginia Bottomley and her colleagues at that time was a serious breach and lack of trust between the Department of Health and the dental profession. It is important to remember here that dentists remained independent practitioners. There was no obligation upon any individual practitioner to devote a minimum proportion of his time to the General Dental Service (the dental arm of the NHS) or indeed to work for it at all. Thus dentists working for the GDS were not salaried employees, but remunerated by prescribed fees for items of treatment, in many cases with a contribution from the patient.

Each year an august body called the Doctors' and Dentists'

Review Body would meet to recommend a "target average net income from General Dental Services for all principals, full time and part-time together, working wholly or partly in these services". The government could accept or vary this proposed target average net income (or TANI) and thereafter a Dental Rates Study Group (DRSG) would forecast an amount for practice expenses, add that amount to TANI to produce a gross amount due to the average dentist, and finally set a fee scale to deliver the amount due, taking account of forecast activity levels but considering also whether to invoke a balancing mechanism to take account of previous under—or over—payments. The breach between the profession and the government had arisen because of the operation of this "claw back" mechanism.

My previous exposure to dentistry had been limited to sessions in the dentist's chair. My first practitioner had been a florid Scotsman, qualified in the days before a university degree was deemed essential. I recall that, at about eighteen years of age, I had called for a check-up after rather a long interval, and in some apprehension that hidden cavities might be discovered and probed. As I sat in his waiting-room, immediately below his surgery on the floor above, I became acutely aware of a series of low moans coming through the ceiling, accompanied by a sinister drumming of heels on the floor. Shortly after this drama ended, I saw through the open door a white-faced woman descending the stairs with a blood-flecked handkerchief pressed to her lips. "Come up, Kenneth," shouted Mr Donaldson from above. I arrived to find him distinctly agitated. "Will you look at that," he said, showing me a perfect set of teeth marks on the back of his hand. "That bloody bitch has nearly bitten me to the bone." Happily, in my own case, all was orally well.

When serving in New York my dentist had the improbable (but rather suitable) name of Dr O E Pick. Happily I never had an experience to match that of Howard Smith, a diplomat posted to Northern Ireland after service as HM Ambassador to Czechoslovakia (and later Director General of MI5). On news of his posting to Prague, and dubious about the possible condition of Czech dentistry, Smith decided to have a dental check of another kind. "I'm so glad you came to see me," said the chosen London practitioner, "because you are bound to have trouble with a really nasty wisdom tooth. Better to have it out now." There then ensued a struggle of gargantuan proportions to prise loose the errant tooth. After what seemed an age the tooth was still only one third out and two thirds in. "I can't go on," cried the practitioner, dropping his instruments of torture into the enamelled bowl. "I've lost my nerve."

I suspect, then, that it was my previous contact with Dr Mawhinney, rather than any prolonged exposure to dental issues, which led to an invitation to conduct what my terms of reference described as "a fundamental review of the existing system of dental remuneration" and to identify "options for change".

However, I was by no means issued with a blank cheque. I was to consider the system but not the level of remuneration, which would continue to rest on the work of the DDRB. Nor was I asked or expected to make a single firm recommendation for change, but rather to discuss and weigh possible alternative options. I would be working with a Panel of Advisors, drawn from government, the NHS and the dental profession, but the ultimate report would be mine and mine alone. Right at the start, I was dismayed by a realisation that the General Dental Services Committee was not the sole voice of the profession, and I was lobbied strongly for representation on the Panel by a rival organisation, the General Dental Practitioners' Association.

I decided early on that I must seek the views of dentists from all parts of the United Kingdom. One means of doing this was through a written request for views from all members of the profession, on the basis of questions which I drew up with the help of the Panel of Advisors. I was, however, anxious to meet dentists face-to-face, to visit their practices and see and discuss their modus operandi. Since there were Health Departments embodied in the Northern Ireland, Scottish and Welsh Offices, I would be reporting to the three "regional" Secretaries of State as well as the Health Secretary.

My visits around the country were deeply informative and sometimes unexpectedly entertaining. The realities of dental (and indeed other) life in deprived areas of Glasgow was brought home to me by a practitioner who complained that local miscreants had made off not just with the brass plate on his door, but with the door itself. Meeting in Cardiff a representative group of Welsh dentists, I had assumed in my naiveté that at a pre-meeting they would have agreed a line to pursue with me. In practice such a vigorous debate ensued—"How can you possibly say that, Gareth, when you know that has never been our policy?"—that I became essentially a spectator at this Cardiff Arms Park of dental rhetoric.

It is not my purpose here to reproduce all the elements of my December 1992 report, which ran to seventy-five pages. I cannot imagine that anyone outside the profession would find it an absorbing read. Obedient to my guidance to produce options rather than make firm recommendations, my principal conclusions remained a little veiled. Now that more than fifteen years have passed, I feel I can indulge myself with a modicum of candour. After presentation of my report, progress was so cautious and glacially slow that I wondered sometimes whether the real motive for appointing me had not been to dampen down the then current controversy. Two aspects of the situation particularly troubled me. One was that we had been seeking to operate a single universal system of remuneration across a number of nations and regions with different dental needs. Conscious as I was (and am) of a conscientious objection to fluoridation of the water supply, I was in no doubt that dental health was much better in areas where this had been done. It also seemed a fundamental weakness of the system, not least in presentational terms, that the NHS fee for a particular item of service was well below that commonly charged for a similar treatment by a dentist in private practice. It was not sufficiently realised that the GDS scale did not work forward from the true cost of an individual treatment, but backwards from the TANI.

Above all, though, I was concerned that the presentation of a universal GDS as part of the National Health Service was a sham. Unless government was prepared to increase substantially the sums available to fund the service, one could see a growing and inevitable withdrawal of practitioners into private practice. Full cover for the elderly, for the impoverished, for children and for a limited range of treatment in other cases could leave room for adequate remuneration to keep sufficient full or part-time dentists within the GDS. I am afraid that subsequent developments have borne out these fears; I myself, like so many others, now look to cover my dental treatment by private insurance.

It was rather intimidating, even for a former civil servant, to present my report to four Secretaries of State around Virginia Bottomley's table. Subsequently, the Health Select Committee of the House of Commons tried very hard to push me beyond the rehearsal of options to a statement of my own preference. I had to tread carefully here, given my terms of reference.

As so often happens, the major issues and suggestions were overtaken by a secondary issue. I was made aware that regular dental attention throughout pregnancy was considered important, and for this reason pregnant women were not asked to pay the private fee which supplemented the government funding per item of service. I dared, then, to suggest that pregnant women well able to afford it should not be subsidised in this way. The consequent reaction reminded me of the late George Thomas's reaction to the furore caused when, as a Junior Home Office Minister, he had referred to Northern Ireland as "the colony". " My, my," he observed, "I wish I hadn't said that."

So this suggestion, tucked away on page thirty-eight of my seventy-five-page report, received more attention than the rest of the report put together. On the very day of its release, an interviewer from our local BBC Radio Ulster interviewed a local mother who had just given birth in the Royal Maternity Hospital. "I see," she said, "that a report today suggests that pregnant women should no longer get free dental treatment. What do you think of that?" "I think it's ridiculous; sure everyone knows free dental treatment is one of the perks of being pregnant."

Later, when being taken over the hurdles of my report by the Health Select Committee, the fierce Labour MP Audrey Wise poured scorn upon this confrontation of the sisterhood. No gentleman would ever attack a pregnant woman in a physical sense; no wise man, I reflected rather too late, would offend her in any other sense.

Nevertheless I had enjoyed the experience. On publication of the report, Jo Rich, who as chairman of the GDSC had served on the Panel of Advisors, was kind enough to write that the task "could not have been done with more sensitivity, integrity and sincerity". Sir Paul Bramley, Emeritus Professor of Dental Surgery at the University of Sheffield, wrote of "the grasp [the report] it shows and the practical wisdom in terms of implementation". I was particularly pleased to have the support of Lord Colwyn, almost certainly the only dental practitioner in the House of Lords, since a previous holder of that title had carried out a landmark review of Northern Ireland's finances in the 1920s.

Nevertheless, I made a covert resolution to stay well away from dentists until the dust of my report had settled. It was not to be. The rugby football team associated with my old school, Instonians, was to compete at home in the All-Ireland League against a team from Munster. The passion for the great game in that part of Ireland has to be seen to be believed. On this occasion bus-loads of fanatical supporters drove up from Limerick, and both outnumbered and out-shouted the more reserved home supporters. Next to me, on the touch-line, stood a Limerick lady with truly impressive lung-power. As her side pulled comfortably ahead of our own, she opted for a friendly gesture. "Here," she said, proferring a large paper bag. "Have a toffee."

In the interests of cross-border harmony and inter-provincial amity I accepted this symbolic peace offering, but at the first chew felt the unmistakeable tug of a previously well-established filling separating from its moorings. So I had to visit my dentist after all; but he was gentle with me. Perhaps he knew that my arguments were already heading for the human equivalent of the elephant's graveyard.

***

In 1993 I became involved in other aspects of the National Health Service. In Northern Ireland there had been successive reorganisations affecting the provision of both primary and secondary medical treatment. In the immediate post-war period, tuberculosis had still been a widespread and much feared disease; I can remember driving past the "TB Sanatorium" at the Forster Green Hospital with a sense of pity and apprehension. In time the creation of a specialised Northern Ireland Tuberculosis Authority, coupled with the effectiveness of new drugs, broke the back of this appalling problem. Then, for a time, a General Health Services Board oversaw primary care in the province, while hospital services were the concern of a Northern Ireland Hospitals Authority (from whose principal medical officer we were to buy our house at Crawfordsburn, later blown up by the IRA). The next phase was the emergence of a series of Area Boards in which health and personal social services were brigaded together; a rational and progressive step, giving us a clear advantage over England in the development of these different modes of care. Now, in 1993, the Area Boards were devolving their operational responsibilities to a series of Trusts. In the case of Hospital Trusts, the Area Boards would be the primary budget holders, and would commission and purchase procedures from the Trusts, which would carry them out. One consequence of this "reform" would be that any hospital providing a regional specialism would find itself involved in contractual negotiations each year with more than one Board, or even with all of them.

I was invited, then, to become a non-executive Board Member of one of these new concerns, the Green Park Healthcare Trust. Unlike Trusts responsible for a single large hospital, such as the Royal Victoria and City Hospitals in Belfast, our new Trust would be responsible for three hospitals on separate sites: the old Musgrave Park Hospital, still using, alongside more modern facilities, temporary buildings dating back to its use as a military hospital during the war; the Belvoir Park Hospital on the "Purdysburn" site where I had been treated for infant scarlet fever; and the old Forster Green Hospital, no longer concerned with the treatment of tuberculosis. We would be responsible, too, for the Joss Cardwell Rehabilitation Centre in East Belfast. We would be the principal regional centre for oncology (both radiotherapy and chemotherapy) at Belvoir Park and for elective orthopaedic surgery at Musgrave Park.

The Chairman of the new Trust would be Norman Shaw, a very well-known figure not just in Northern Irish but in UK agriculture, and other non-executive colleagues would include Viscount Brookeborough, grandson of the former Northern Ireland Prime Minister, and Ian Doherty of Derry, who had shared rooms at Cambridge with Michael Portillo. The executive members were headed by our very efficient Chief Executive, Hilary Boyd, with the leading orthopaedic surgeon, James Nixon, as our first Medical Director. I am happy to say that, from beginning to end, the non-executives, the administrative staff and the clinicians and nurses worked well and harmoniously together, which was not always the case in other parts of the United Kingdom.

In many ways Musgrave Park was the jewel in our crown— one of the largest centres for elective orthopaedic surgery in the whole of Europe, and with its own mini-factory to produce customised hip-joints. My own father, at a great age, had benefited enormously from their skills and experience.

However, some major issues of concern emerged during my four-year term on the Board. Contract negotiations with the several Area Boards could be so complex and protracted that one would be deep into a new financial year before having any certainty about the funds available. This presented an invidious choice between slowing down throughput early in the year, and working facilities and clinicians to death later on to use the available money, or working flat out early on and applying the brakes abruptly towards the end of the year. Since we clearly needed more operating theatres, more orthopaedic surgeons, more anaesthetists, more nurses and other staff to keep waiting lists at a tolerable level, it seemed a great pity not to be confident about optimum use of what we had. A close relative, complaining that a patient suffering pain and loss of mobility was having to wait a long time for treatment, would sometimes lay the blame at the feet of the treatment centre. Yet, in truth, we had to live within our means and could only carry out procedures commissioned and paid for by an Area Board.

We also found ourselves, during my time as a Board Member, at the centre of a highly important debate about cancer treatment. Definitive research in England, by Sir Kenneth Calman and others, had reached the not very surprising conclusion that the best outcomes were obtained where a patient could be treated by a clinician dealing with high volume of cases of that specific cancer. Moreover, as more "heroic" treatments became available, such as the use of very powerful and expensive but effective drugs, there were strong arguments for embedding cancer treatment in a large hospital capable of dealing with diverse secondary conditions. Work in Northern Ireland itself by Dr Henrietta Campbell, the Chief Medical Officer, argued the case for a brand-new, state-of-the-art cancer centre close to other supportive medical facilities. As Directors of the Green Park Trust, we were proud of the work carried out at Belvoir Park, amidst tranquil surroundings and with wonderful voluntary support from an organisation of Friends. Nevertheless we were persuaded, after agonising debate, to support the project to construct a new Cancer Centre at the Belfast City Hospital, and to facilitate the transition by an earlier transfer of responsibility for treatment, while it continued at Belvoir, to the City Hospital Trust.

One of our first duties as Directors of the new Trust had been to decide how our staff should be paid. With expert consultancy advice, we decided to provide for an element of performance-related pay, and set the basic pay scales at a level taking account of this element in the remuneration system. We were, then, appalled to be told several years into the operation by the Junior Minister then overseeing the Department of Health that Boards were not to award any performance pay. Our view, supported by legal advice, was that we had contractual obligations, the abandonment of which could expose us to legal action. The unhelpful guidance from the Department was that a performance pay scheme implied the right not to pay any in a particular year. For our part we pointed out that the relevant legislation included power for the Minister to issue a binding statutory direction to the Trust. This would be his decision, not ours; let him give his statutory direction and defend it. The Minister and Department were clearly unwilling to do so; we stuck to our guns and took a modest degree of flack from the Comptroller and Auditor General. I still think we were treated in a scandalously authoritarian way, and it was no occasion of sadness when the minister concerned moved on to other things.

In spite of such frustrations, service on a Trust had been a life-enhancing experience. There will always be complaints about the NHS, but I continue to believe that it offers incalculable benefits to society. It may be difficult at times to see the chosen GP in a group practice, and hospital waiting lists are too long. Without a massive incursion of nursing staff from places like the Philippines, it would be almost impossible to cope. I fear, too, that we enjoy today a poorer health service than many other parts of the United Kingdom. Yet, for a person such as myself in my eighth decade, there remains much to admire and be grateful for.

3

Education: To Seek the Truth

LIKE SO MANY OTHERS, I LOOK to my good fortune in the education I received as the foundation for anything I was able to achieve in later life. At the primary level, the old Public Elementary Schools of Belfast gave me a good grounding (and rather beautiful handwriting which I have sadly lost); and it was of course a great privilege later on to read Modern History at Oxford, our country's oldest university. That antiquity, though, was put into a better perspective when a holiday in Morocco took us to Fez, whose venerable university predates that of Oxford by some hundreds of years.

Yet I do not look either to Elementary School or to Oxford as the key educational experience of my life. In his dedication to his *Oxford Book of English Verse*, Sir Arthur Quiller-Couch had spoken of his old college as "ancient, liberal, humane and my most kindly nurse". I would find all of these qualities at "Inst", the Royal Belfast Academical Institution, in which I studied from 1943 to 1949. It was not ancient to the degree of a venerable Oxford College; nevertheless the impulse for its foundation had come from a Belfast radicalism influenced by the French Revolution and dedicated to the wider interests of Ireland. Liberal it had always been, as evidenced by the remarkable

[73]

speech made in 1814 by one of its founding fathers, Dr William Drennan. After the acerbities of the Elementary system, with its continuing emphasis on regular corporal punishment, Inst was conspicuously humane, confining its punishments to nothing more severe than post-school "detention", or the imposition of lines. Summary jurisdiction for minor offences rested with the company of school prefects, and I can still remember the quotation from Dickens spoken by a prefectorial colleague as a tiny malefactor stood before us: "This boy will be hanged. I know this boy will be hanged."

In 1984 I was invited to become one of the Governors of the school, and in that "new life" of which I spoke at Stormont in 1991, I have served first of all as Convenor of the School Committee (concerned with academic performance, senior teaching appointments, etc), and since late 2004, as Chairman of the Board. The invitation to serve in that capacity came as a total surprise. My predecessor, Dr Bob Rodgers, had immense experience of education as the head of prestigious schools and ultimately of Stranmillis College, which trains many of our local teachers; he was recognised as a leading authority; he was of much the same age as myself; and, frankly, I had expected him to remain in post as Chairman until I myself might be ready to retire from the Board. It has always been a problem to attract younger men or women in mid-career to take on these responsibilities and, indeed, twice during my time as a Board member we had celebrated the 90th birthday of a serving colleague! Most of us were there as "representative Governors", elected by members of the Institution for a set term, in practice normally renewed. We had some limited powers of cooption, and a more recent obligation to include Governors elected by the teaching staff and by parents. Since half the parents, even in a boys' school, are women, one effect of this was to bring women to the Board table to the great benefit of the Governors and the school.

Many schools appoint chairpersons for set terms, some of

them comparatively brief, but for whatever reason Inst has established a precedent of very lengthy tenure of the Chair. Dr Rodgers himself had served for seven years, and his predecessor, Sir Robert Carswell (now, as Lord Carswell, one of the Law Lords), for eleven years. When, through "the usual channels" (amounting to soundings amongst senior colleagues), I was asked whether I would allow my name to go forward, I experienced a strange mixture of exhilaration and anxiety. Already well into my seventies, I was thinking in terms of reducing rather than increasing my commitments. It would not be helpful to accept the role and then abandon it after a short time, but as an historian I was conscious of the exciting prospect of our bicentenary in 2010, two hundred years after the establishment of the Institution by Act of Parliament. Above all, though, I was conscious of the huge debt of gratitude I owed to Inst. I felt an obligation to repay it in some small degree, if I could. After all, the motto of the city of Belfast, "Pro tanto quid retribuamus", asks us how much we give back for all we have received. The motto of the school itself, "quaerere verum", enjoined us all to "seek the truth".

My tenure got off to an unfortunate start. Elizabeth and I had been looking forward very much to a short holiday break in Tuscany, but a few days before our intended departure, and half-way up the stairs to change for a formal dinner, I felt a disc pop out of my back. As a result I spent the next couple of weeks not amongst poppies, olive groves and vineyards, but flat on my back in that very Musgrave Park Hospital on whose Trust Board I had served. It was an embarrassment to miss the Governors' meeting at which I was nominated and elected, as well as the senior prize day at which I would normally have presided.

As I returned to something approaching normal, I found myself drawn into an educational maelstrom. In 2000, the Labour government had appointed a committee, chaired by Gerry Burns, a former Northern Ireland Ombudsman (and an old friend and colleague at the Chief Executives' Forum and elsewhere) to make recommendations about the future arrangements for post-primary education. After almost forty years of experience as a civil servant, I well knew that, while governments looked for men and women of intelligence and integrity to serve on such advisory bodies, they were unlikely to appoint many known to be antipathetic to their preconceived ideas. Significantly the senior specialist advisor to the Review Group, Professor Gallagher of Queen's University, was known to be ill-disposed to the long-standing system of academic selection. This was ground we had been over before. In the Seventies, only the defeat of the Labour government of the day had averted the introduction into Northern Ireland of the system of comprehensive education favoured by such as Lord Melchett.

It was, then, no great surprise that the Burns Report of 2002 did not merely recommend the abolition of the unpopular "eleven plus" method of academic selection, but argued for the displacement of all selection on academic grounds in favour of so-called "parental choice".

Since I had been the permanent head of various government departments receiving reports from advisory groups, and indeed had in retirement served on or chaired such groups, I was familiar with the usual protocol. This was that the group concerned would send its report to the responsible minister, commonly explain the broad thrust of its recommendations on the day of publication, and then disband, leaving it to the commissioning department to carry forward any consultative process and reach final decisions.

I was more than surprised, then, that Burns and colleagues were sent around the country as a kind of "road show", not so much explaining their recommendations as selling them, with Professor Gallagher to the fore and the Department of Education clearly in support.

There was, however, some apparent degree of reassurance in the Department's undertaking to explore reaction to the issues presented by Burns through a "household survey" which, we were proudly told, would be one of the most comprehensive consultative exercises ever carried out by government in Northern Ireland. The two major issues, alongside others of lesser importance, were these: did the people of Northern Ireland wish to discontinue the "eleven plus" tests as the basis for academic selection for post-primary education; and, in the absence of the "eleven plus", did they favour the retention of some alternative basis of academic selection?

The consultative exercise was indeed comprehensive, extensive and, incidentally, expensive (£419,000). Well over 200,000 households responded, including 162,000 parents and 21,000 teachers. There were convincing majorities favouring abolition of the "eleven plus"; but there were equally substantial majorities favouring the retention of academic selection in some form.

Although the Burns Report had been commissioned by the Labour administration under the system of direct rule, the decision-making power had passed on devolution to the Executive's Minister of Education, Martin McGuinness of Sinn Féin, who had set the consultative process in train. Significantly, when just about half the responses had been received, the Minister had observed, "I have 100,000 responses sitting in my Department and these are the people that count."

Unfortunately the Minister himself seemed unable or unwilling to count the very large number of respondents who had expressed support for the principle of academic selection. On virtually his last day in office before the Assembly imploded and direct rule was re-introduced, McGuinness announced that in future no consideration of academic criteria would be permitted in selection for post-primary education; the paramount principle would be "parental choice".

When the Assembly collapsed, it was very understandable that direct rule ministers could not tolerate an indefinite policy and legislative vacuum. No one could be sure whether, or when, the Humpty Dumpty of the Good Friday Agreement could be put together again. Nor would the Treasury wait forever for measures to contain demands on the national Exchequer. There was, then, an underlying disposition to carry into effect decisions already taken in principle by the local Executive.

However, I must return here to the issue which had come to the fore in our review of Jersey's government. In a conventional well-functioning democracy, a minister making a radical declaration of new policy would be expected to seek and gain the agreement of his cabinet colleagues and to take account of his ability to give that declaration legislative effect. Neither of these conditions was met by McGuinness's decree that academic selection should be abolished. The Northern Ireland Executive had not operated on the basis of collective responsibility as commonly understood, and if McGuinness's proposals had been put to the test under the stringent arrangements requiring broad consensus arising from the Good Friday Agreement, they would certainly have failed to achieve sufficient support to be passed into law by the Assembly.

The new direct rule Minister, Jane Kennedy, then appointed a further committee chaired by Steve Costello to carry the alleged "reforms" a stage further. It was from the outset not only foreseeable but inevitable that the Costello Report would carry forward the thrust of the Burns/McGuinness proposals.

When I succeeded Bob Rodgers as Chairman of the Inst Board, I also replaced him on the Executive Committee of the Governing Bodies Association (GBA), and found that its representatives had been in prolonged dialogue with the Department of Education and successive ministers. They had been given assurances that there was no intention, in these prospective "reforms", to abolish grammar schools, to impose the comprehensive system in Northern Ireland, or to seek a "one size fits all" solution. GBA representatives had pointed out that "parental choice" implied that a child would be guaranteed a place in the school chosen by his or her parents. Since many schools would undoubtedly be over-subscribed, this would by no means be the case. Moreover, "parental choice", or, in reality, "parental preference" could only be effective if one could be confident of informed choice or preference. Yet it seemed that potential receiving schools would be afforded no assured role in offering guidance, let alone in making final judgments of suitability. If all schools were not over time to become much the same in character, the aim should surely be to facilitate the most comfortable and appropriate "fit" between child and school. There would be a so-called "pupil profile" recording a child's progress through primary school, but there were fears that this would exclude hard and reliable data permitting effective assessment and comparison. There was also the prospect of an extraordinarily extensive curriculum whose main covert purpose seemed to be to undermine the viability of smaller schools in the interests of rationalising the school estate. The GBA saw a future in which geographical proximity to a school would be a major determinant of entry, with the very possible consequences of encouraging some schools to go independent and driving up property prices around "good schools".

None of the responses from the Department showed any willingness to respond in a meaningful way to the GBA's concerns. As I began to attend meetings, not only of the Executive Committee but of the wider Association, I became aware of some emerging divisions in the "grammar school constituency". Governors and heads of the numerous (and academically excellent) Catholic schools, particularly those under diocesan control, were under pressure from the hierarchy, and in particular, Bishop Donal McKeown, a former President of St Malachy's College, to go along with the proposed "reforms" in the interests of social justice and cohesion. I found it hard to reconcile this with my knowledge that the Northern Ireland system could show much the best results in the whole United Kingdom in terms of preparing children from less affluent backgrounds for university education. There were those who, while admitting that patient negotiation had achieved little by way of concession so far, continued to believe it offered the best prospects of preserving the virtues of academic education. There were pessimists—some would say defeatists—who argued that the abolition of academic selection was a "done deal" and that our focus should be on making the best of the new system, for instance in terms of allowable criteria for entry. Finally I could identify a faction—which at first seemed undesirably strident— who argued for much more vigorous, vociferous and public opposition to the government's proposals.

For me the moment of truth came with the publication of a draft Education (Northern Ireland) Order 2006. A draft Instrument of this kind would commonly allow a very limited time for consideration and comment, and the probability was that it would be introduced into Parliament by the middle of the year. In my view we were now facing grievous damage to a system of academic education which has served Northern Ireland well for generations. More or less spontaneously, but owing not a little to the commitment of Bill Young, head of Belfast Royal Academy, a group of school governors, head teachers, former pupils and concerned parents came together to decide what urgent action could be taken at this very late stage.

The decision was to launch a new "umbrella body" to be called the Association for Quality Education, and to place advertisements inviting supporters to subscribe to a "fighting fund" for further action. Because of my experience in government, and because much of the effort would have to be directed at Parliament, I was invited to serve as Chairman of the AQE and to act as its principal spokesman. In a short time we raised a "fighting fund" of some £40,000 and were able to include in our campaign a well-attended and enthusiastic rally in Belfast's historic Ulster Hall. On that day I included in my remarks the following:

We meet today to express our deep concern about two matters of incalculable importance to us all—not just to those who join us in this historic Hall today, but all of us who live in Northern Ireland, and indeed generations yet to come.

In one sense this Ulster Hall is a place full of ghosts; of echoes of past causes and past struggles. Our focus today is on issues every bit as profound and long-lasting. For we have met to speak of the education of our children, and of our determination to enjoy equal citizenship and proper democratic rights within this United Kingdom. We seek to avert measures which could affect the lives of our children and our children's children.

I speak to you as Chairman of the Association for Quality Education and also of the Governors of Inst, a school which has been proud of its ethos and achievements for almost two hundred years. I owe an incalculable debt not only to that great school, which I attended in the Forties, but also to the Public Elementary system in which I began my education. I have not come here today to claim perfection for all our current educational arrangements. We well know that in parts of this city, beset for too long by social, economic and public order problems, bright children and dedicated teachers struggle to cope. Nor have I come here to claim that, at the secondary level, grammar schools are the sole centres of excellence. One could not—as I have done—visit a school like St Louise's [Comprehensive College on Belfast's Falls Road] without experiencing profound admiration for its ethos and achievements.

But pause a moment to consider the strengths of what we have. In a mixed economy of schools—public and voluntary; single sex and co-educational; church-based or secular or integrated—we achieve remarkable results, at GCSE, at A level, and at entry into third-level education. From its earliest days in office, the Blair government has set great store on the objective of getting more of our young people, and in particular our young people from less-privileged backgrounds, into the universities. And where, I ask you, has that objective been most fully realised? The answer is, here in Northern Ireland. One has not, so far, to secure entry for one's child to a school of choice, had to buy an expensive place in some pricey independent school or pay inflated house prices to live in a particular neighbourhood which is the catchment area for a favoured school.

Our Association—bringing together head teachers, school governors, old pupils and parents—came into being because months and years of patient dialogue between the Governing Bodies Association and Government had yielded no concession of any real value to our deep concern. We had reached the stage of publication of a draft Order in Council which, if carried into law, would effectively prohibit forever any assessment of academic ability or aptitude as a criterion for entry into schools hitherto rooted in academic rigour; and this in spite of repeated assurances that such proposals represented no threat to our grammar schools, no intention to introduce comprehensive education, no "one size fits all" solution. Ministers offered assurance, but we were not reassured. We were indignant that, while six separate tests of opinion had shown a majority of respondents favouring retention of some form of academic selection, these clear expressions of opinion had fallen upon deaf ears.

So it was that we decided that, if we were to be heard even at this late stage, we must raise our voices. And so, with generous support from many who believe in our cause, we are mounting a campaign which reaches its culmination in this rally today. We have placed newspaper advertisements, addressed political groupings when invited to do so, and lobbied in both Houses of Parliament. There have been face to face encounters with the Prime Minister himself and with Angela Smith, and Peter Hain [NI Secretary of State] has agreed to meet me to hear our representations. [I note in parenthesis that he made such a meeting conditional on my first seeing his Education Minister, Angela Smith. While I contacted his office as soon as that condition had been met, I was unimpressed by the fact that he only saw me after the Order had passed through both Houses.] I have debated the government's proposals at the Belfast City Hall with Martin McGuinness, and what an irony it was to hear him express his concern about under-performance on the Shankill! I found it strange that a party whose raison d'etre is to remove British influence from Ireland should voice such enthusiasm for the imposition by a British government of a policy so obviously unwanted by a majority of the local community.

To members of both Houses of Parliament who have been willing to meet us we have presented a democratic argument which should weigh even with those not well-disposed to academic selection. Let me repeat for you the essence of our case. First of all, the view of the

[82]

local community is clear and unmistakable. Never in my lifetime have I experienced a British government so keen on consultative exercises, "grand conversations", focus groups. When the response of our people is that they do not care for the "eleven plus" method of selection, this is happily accepted as validation. But when a further response is that a majority wants an alternative basis for academic selection, this is brushed aside.

Second, let us recall the origin of this obnoxious policy. As virtually his last act in office, Martin McGuinness, as outgoing Minister of Education, decreed that academic selection should be barred. When direct rule had to be resumed, there was a disposition to carry on with decisions already taken by the Northern Ireland Executive. But let us be clear about this. Mr McGuinness spoke not for the Executive but for himself and his party. He had not sought the consent of other colleagues; he did not have the backing of the Assembly.

That Assembly was operating within the rules and procedures put in place by the Good Friday Agreement. Under those rules a contentious and divisive proposal could only have been carried into law with both majority and cross-party support. I tell you this with absolute certainty; proposals such as those embodied in the current draft Order would never have been passed by the Assembly, nor would they be passed in a recalled Assembly using its law-making powers. "Ah, yes," ministers may say, "but in the absence of an Assembly we have to do what we think best." But pause a moment. government tells us again and again that the essential elements of the Good Friday Agreement are non-negotiable. And so I ask the question: if it is good in Northern Ireland to seek consensus and avoid divisive measures, why is it acceptable for a British government as caretaker to set that precept aside?

If the changes envisaged by the current Order are put into place, I fear that too many parents—guided only by a so-called "pupil profile" of limited value, and under no obligation even to invite advice from a receiving school—may make choices not in the best interests of their child.

In such an atmosphere, those rated "good schools" by popular opinion could be massively over-subscribed, and vicinity to the school could become a principal determinant of entry. Social and geographical mixing would be undermined; over time money would replace merit. People in rural areas could find themselves greatly limited in their choice of school." "Parental choice" would prove a misnomer; "parental preference" could only be effective if based on reliable information and a choice between truly acceptable options.

Let us, then, send a strong, clear and unmistakable message to government today. Do not ignore the opinion of the local community; do not rush to take decisions best left to those we choose to represent us; resolve, by all means, to strengthen our system of education where you can, but appreciate that the worst possible start would be to damage one of its strongest parts.

It soon became clear that our cause would attract valuable political support, both locally and nationally. I could never have been counted as a sympathizer with the DUP, and was therefore surprised to be invited with some others to speak about the current education issues at the party's forthcoming Annual Conference. Whatever my own political views, I could not in good conscience miss an opportunity to put our case to a party now enjoying significant representation in Parliament. When I arrived at the Ramada Hotel, the Conference was running behind schedule, and so I had the entertainment of listening to a speech by Sammy Wilson, which was a minor masterpiece of scathing humour. The large attendance and the professionalism of the conference arrangements showed a party in good heart and good order. When the time came, my speech was well received, in particular my concluding remarks: "Having spent almost forty years saying, 'Yes, minister' what a treat it is to be able to say 'No, minister'."

In the following week we had made plans to visit Westminster, but it was a great surprise to learn from DUP sources that they had secured for Bill Young and myself an opportunity for a short meeting with the Prime Minister. This took place in Blair's modest office at the House of Commons. It was a surreal experience to find oneself sitting next to the Prime Minister on the celebrated sofa, with Bill Young and Sammy Wilson opposite and the PPS taking a note. Tony Blair, I thought, when seen from close up, looked rather tired and strained. We had adequate time to put our points and received a polite hearing but, as we would have expected, no specific response. As we emerged from this meeting, the ante-room next door was seething with attendees for his next meeting—John Prescott, Des Browne (then Chief Secretary at the Treasury), and a horde of more anonymous people, I suspect concerned with some issue of public expenditure. One had a revelation of a typical Prime Minister's day, bouncing hour after hour from one meeting to another, from one topic to another.

The Unionist Party were also directly supportive. David McNarry, their education spokesman, invited me to join an education seminar at Stormont, addressed not only by the party leader, Reg Empey, but by the Conservative spokesman on Northern Ireland, David Lidington, who had flown from London specifically for the occasion.

Thereafter, with colleagues or on my own, I made several further visits to Westminster, discussing our problem with my old ministerial chief Tom King (now Lord King of Bridgewater) and meeting a range of parliamentarians from the Conservative and Liberal Democrat parties, as well as cross-bench peers in the House of Lords. Our aim throughout was to persuade ministers to withdraw or amend the proposed legislation, to illustrate and stimulate the degree of local opposition to it, and to exploit the possibility of rejection of the Order in the House of Lords if the government proceeded with it unamended. I had a particularly useful and interesting encounter with a substantial group of cross-bench peers. Until my involvement in our campaign I had not appreciated that the cross-bench peers, who cannot be "whipped" in any conventional sense, nevertheless choose a convenor, at that time Lord Williamson of Horton. Looking him up in *Who's Who* I realised he was the David Williamson I had met from time to time years before, when he was Secretary-General of the European Commission. In a letter to him I said that I understood cross-bench peers would sometimes admit an outsider to one of their periodic meetings to speak about an issue of current importance. To my great satisfaction, I was accorded an opportunity to do this on 17 May 2006.

This was to be an event in an unusual week. On the Monday, as guests at the Secretary of State's annual Garden Party at Hillsborough Castle, Elizabeth and I had been able to meet and chat to the Duchess of Cornwall, accompanying her husband, the Prince of Wales. We travelled to London on the Tuesday to attend the following day the quadrennial service of the Order of the Bath at Westminster Abbey, in which senior members of the Grand Cross of the Order are installed with great ceremony in the presence of the Queen and the Prince of Wales, who is Great Master of the Order. It was a morning of British pageantry at its best; scarlet-cloaked Field Marshals wielding their batons, State trumpeters, Yeomen of the Guard, the clink-clink of the spurs of the Gentlemen at Arms, trumpet calls, organ music and wonderful choral singing. As a relatively senior KCB I found myself seated in the choir-stalls next to two figures from an earlier life, a former Treasury Solicitor and a former Governor of Jersey at the time of the Clothier Review.

Removing my rather showy star of the Bath, but still in full morning dress, Elizabeth and I crossed the road from the Abbey to the House of Lords for lunch with two of the Northern Ireland peers, Lords Laird and Rogan, and Lord Williamson himself. I was extremely pleased to see at the subsequent meeting some " heavy hitters" such as Elspeth Howe (Baroness Howe of Idlicote), wife of Geoffrey Howe, and Patrick Wright (Lord Wright of Richmond), a former Head of the Diplomatic Service. Next day we were to attend the Queen's reception at Buckingham Palace.

It was clear to us in our encounters with politicians that many of them were not antipathetic in principle to comprehensive education. It was necessary, therefore, not to rest our case solely on the merits of our grammar schools, and to emphasize our concern for the welfare of non-academic as well as academic children. At the heart of the matter was the proposal to write into law a provision that criteria for entry into any post-primary school should not include the academic aptitude or ability of a child (whether assessed by reference to his or her performance in any test or examination or by any means whatever).

The significance of this provision becomes clear when one compares the legislative procedures which applied at Westminster under direct rule with those which would apply in an active Northern Ireland Assembly. The Order in Council procedure for Northern Ireland legislation was first introduced when William Whitelaw arrived as the first Secretary of State. Each year the old Stormont Parliament had been passing thirty or more local Acts applying to Northern Ireland alone, by means similar to those in the Westminster Parliament: in each House introduction or First Reading; Second Reading with ample debate of broad principles; Committee Stage with clause-by-clause consideration and room for amendment; and Report Stage with yet further possibility to amend. There was clearly no prospect of finding room in the Westminster parliamentary programme for this high volume of specifically Northern Irish legislation. So, as a temporary device during what was hoped to be a relatively brief interregnum before the restoration of a new Northern Ireland legislature, the Order in Council procedure was put in place. A draft Statutory Instrument, if approved by resolution in each House of Parliament, would become law as an Order made by the Queen in Council. Under this procedure, debate would be limited, and the only option open to either House would be to accept or reject the Order as a whole. No amendments could be introduced or carried. This procedure, intended to be a short-term expedient, was now being used more than thirty years later to enact controversial legislation which in any part of Great Britain, whether at Westminster, in the Scottish Parliament in Edinburgh or the Welsh Assembly in Cardiff, would be open to prolonged debate and possible amendment in the legislature.

The irony is that, for a devolved Northern Ireland, the bar had been set higher than this. The negotiating parties for the Good Friday Agreement—including, of course, the government bringing forward the draft Education Order—agreed that there must be a mechanism in any Northern Ireland Assembly to prevent passage of controversial and potentially divisive legislation by a simple majority. Thus a number of Assembly members could trigger by petition a requirement for cross-community as well as overall majority support. The legislation binding a Northern Ireland Assembly did not, of course, bind Parliament, and in the narrow legal sense a government was entitled to behave as it wished. But in the wider moral sense, it was difficult to see that the avoidance of profoundly divisive measures was of no account in a situation of direct rule.

Until the draft Order was finally laid before Parliament, we retained a hope that the House of Lords would not accept it. We had the firm backing of the Conservative peers, and a hope that some of the cross-benchers had been moved by our arguments. The vital "swing vote" might well rest with the Liberal Democrats. We were, of course, well aware that some members of that party—for example Shirley Williams—were firm believers in the comprehensive system and opposed to academic selection. With them we rested our case on the democratic argument; that a government proposed to impose on Northern Ireland, by truncated legislative procedures, radical changes in the education system against the clear wishes of a majority of those who would be affected by them. We knew that Lord Smith of Clifton, previously a Vice Chancellor in Northern Ireland, was deeply uneasy about the Order in Council procedure. We had seen correspondence from the then party leader, Sir Menzies Campbell, accepting that local opinion favoured academic selection, that such an important issue should not be decided upon by politicians at Westminster who were not democratically accountable to the people of Northern Ireland, and expressing opposition to such a policy change being made by means of an Order in Council.

How, then, did it come about that when the draft Order came before the House of Lords on 10 July the Liberal Democrats aligned themselves with the Labour peers in voting approval? One must be blunt; they fell hook, line and sinker for a ploy put into play by Peter Hain. He was prepared, he announced, to stay the abandonment of academic selection until the expiry in November of the deadline set for the full restoration of the devolved institutions. If, by then, a local Assembly returned to full operation, the decision about selection would be left to them. Many of us regarded this as a pretty cynical exercise. If it was wrong and undemocratic to use truncated process to impose unwanted change in July, it would be no more acceptable and democratic in November.

What we had, then, was a piece of legislation to which a majority of Northern Ireland people were opposed, as shown by no fewer than six government or other surveys, brought forward by a governing party which does not put up a single candidate in Northern Ireland, and at a time when the then Prime Minister himself had disavowed any wish to "take on" those remaining grammar schools in England which continued to exist with strong local support. The idea of "specialist schools" supposedly to be available in Northern Ireland as in Great Britain, seemed to be a nonsense if applicants to, say, a specialist music school could not be asked to give any evidence of musical aptitude or ability.

However, things "changed utterly" with the restoration of devolution to an Executive and Assembly dominated by the DUP and Sinn Féin. Once again, in the rotational system for the allocation of ministerial places, the Department of Education came under the ministerial control of Sinn Féin, this time in the person of Catríona Ruane. But things had changed since Martin McGuinness had been in a position to make a wholly unilateral declaration. The St Andrew's Agreement had added to the requirement for consensus in legislation a matching obligation to seek consensus in executive decisions. AQE were afforded an opportunity to put our case to the Assembly Education Committee (chaired by Sammy Wilson of the DUP) and were invited by the minister to put our proposals to her. We have worked very hard to develop potential methods of academic selection which take account of legitimate criticisms of the "eleven plus". It still seems best to us that the capacity of children should be assessed within the primary system, not to distinguish "successes" from "failures", but to enable each individual child to be matched to the type of school best suited to his or her talents, capabilities and interests. We seek to avoid as far as possible "coaching" or other means favouring middle-class over working-class children. But if all concerned cannot co-operate in developing a widely acceptable system of "exit tests" undertaken within the primary school, schools wishing to preserve academic criteria may wish to mount tests of their own or to join with others in a common testing system. We continue to believe that a shift towards neighbourhood comprehensive schools would work to the disadvantage of able children from underprivileged backgrounds, and replace merit with money as a means to secure entry to the most popular and successful schools. Those of us, like myself, who availed of a ladder up which we could climb to academic and professional opportunities unavailable to our parents do not want to see that ladder kicked away before our rising generation.

***

As if the conduct of the AQE campaign were not enough, I found myself faced, as a new chairman at Inst, with the most important issue confronted by any Board of Governors, the choice of a new Principal or Head. Quite soon after I assumed the chair, the incumbent Principal, Michael Ridley, who had led the school with real distinction since 1990, indicated to me that he was contemplating retirement on or about the time of his sixtieth birthday, in January 2007. After taking some senior Board members into my confidence, I asked Michael to think it over during the summer vacation of 2005, in discussion with his wife Jenny, who had been such a support to him during his time at Inst. When we returned to the matter at the start of a new school year, Michael reaffirmed his view that he should retire at the end of 2006. He thought that, in many ways, the end of the first term might be a better time to leave than the end of the school year. The important decisions for the rest of the year would have been taken, and a successor would have the time and space to look around before plotting any new course.

Colleagues were informed of Michael's decision at the December 2005 meeting of the Board, and we then applied ourselves with some urgency to the logistics of replacement. We hoped to attract applications from serving Heads of other schools, and since such an applicant, if successful, would want to give his or her current employer due notice to allow time to appoint a successor, it was clear that we must aim to complete our appointment process by Easter 2006. In making the necessary arrangements with the School Committee, where Brian Hanna, former Chief Executive of Belfast City Council, had succeeded me as convenor, we had to settle how and where to advertise, what terms to offer and agree a firm timeline for advertisement, expressions of interest, supply of full particulars to respondents, decisions as to whether any candidates failed to meet prescribed essential criteria, the taking up of references for candidates still in the field, and finally two rounds of interviews. The School Committee, chaired for this purpose by myself as chairman rather than by the convenor, would interview all the candidates meeting the essential criteria. They would be asked, first of all, to give a relatively brief presentation on lines outlined in advance, and thereafter I would ask each to respond to a series of questions, again agreed in advance. Thereafter we would consider the credentials of each candidate in the round; their CV, the quality of their presentation, their reaction to the questions put to them, and the nature of their references. (Candidates will never invite someone who does not think well of them to act as a referee, but on occasions reservations can be read "between the lines".) Our objective would be to identify for final interview by the whole Board next day only candidates who could, if appointed, credibly lead the school. Because we hoped to attract applicants from Great Britain, as well as from Northern Ireland, including senior members of our own staff, we did not wish to find ourselves in the position of offering the post to a candidate whose wife, husband or partner had never set foot in Northern Ireland. To avoid the risk of someone feeling they could only accept provisionally, we decided to invite applicants from outside Northern Ireland to bring their wives, husbands or partners with them, and to hold a social event on the Friday evening— that is to say after completion of the first round of interviews— for candidates, spouses or partners and Board members with their wives to meet each other. This would emphatically not be an element in the selection process itself; one did not propose to "vet" wives as if this were an old-style Tory selection meeting for a parliamentary candidate.

Clearly, though, a blight would be cast over the occasion if some of the candidates had already been told that they had not been chosen for further interview. We would, therefore, meet briefly in School Committee early on the Saturday morning, firm up, or probably reaffirm, our judgments of the day before, and I would then tell the rest of the Board our recommendations for further interview. Thereafter I would have the painful duty of telling the unsuccessful, and the pleasant duty of telling the successful, what the Board, on our recommendation, had decided. The full Board would then hear the same presentation made by a candidate the day before, and thereafter candidates would be asked to respond to further questions from pre-selected senior Governors not involved at the first stage.

Our fear as we embarked on the process was that, given the prevailing uncertainty about the future of academic selection, there would be little interest from schools "across the water". It seemed more likely that, in these circumstances, the position would have greater appeal to head teachers or others already in Northern Ireland and wishing to stay there. We knew that some very good local schools had experienced real difficulty in attracting a good field, and by chance a number of existing Northern Ireland heads were approaching retirement.

It goes without saying that, in compliance with the law, and for wholly practical reasons, all our procedures had been intentionally gender-neutral. We had for almost two hundred years been a school only for boys, but we had been strengthened by the presence of female governors and were well aware of the increasingly strong representation of women within the teaching profession. Not long before we had appointed Dr Caroline Greer to one of the most senior positions in the school as head of the Science Department, and been greatly impressed by her energy, enthusiasm and imagination in this key post.

Happily, our fears that we would attract a sub-standard field in the prevailing conditions of uncertainty were not realised, and we were able to identify six good candidates who fully met the criteria and were accordingly invited to appear before the School Committee for a first interview. These six included three from Great Britain, two serving heads and a sole woman.

Needless to say, I was conscious of the crucial importance of the process. On his retirement Michael Ridley would have served the school for some sixteen years, and we were now looking for a successor who could steer us through to our 2010 bicentenary and beyond, coping in the process with such changes as government or society might impose upon us. Unhappily I went off to the first round of interviews with a nasty bout of the flu, stuffed with pills and in peril of losing my voice. I coped as best I could with interviewing the six candidates, and in our discussions after they had been completed there was an emerging consensus that we should recommend that the full Board grant a final interview to three of the candidates, a senior master from England, our own senior Vice Principal and the head of Antrim Grammar, a Miss Janet Williamson.

I had been looking forward to a chat with candidates and their partners at the social evening we had arranged in the school's splendid Christ Church building, a derelict church brought back to life as a state-of-the-art library and IT centre, with the professional support of Dawson Stelfox, old boy of the school, the first Irishman to climb Mount Everest and a restoration architect of distinction. Unhappily, when I got home from the interviews, I was feeling so wretched that I feared I would have to cry off the following day if I did not retire to bed. I encouraged my wife Elizabeth to go, to make my apologies to our guests, and was pleased to hear on her return that it had been a successful, relaxed and enjoyable evening.

It did not take long the next morning to confirm our provisional conclusions, and on reporting to the full Board we agreed to interview again the three recommended candidates. I then had the task of telling each of the six candidates in turn what we had decided, with the sort of disappointed or exhilarated reactions to be expected.

The chosen three, each in turn, repeated their prepared presentations and responded to questions from my nominated colleagues. I hope it was a relief for candidates to hear some new voices, and as mine had almost disappeared overnight I was glad that we had made this arrangement. At the completion of the interviews, and after time for reflection, we distributed voting papers asking each Governor to rate candidates in order of preference. Two of our convenors took these papers away to the Registrar's office to act as tellers, and sent for me to join them when their work had been completed and scrupulously cross-checked. The result was a mould-breaking event in the long, distinguished history of the school, since the decision of the Board was that the post of Principal should be offered to Miss Janet Williamson.

I am, perhaps, an emotional person, and I had found the

conduct of this vitally important process while far from well quite a strain; so I have to admit that I announced the outcome to my Board colleagues with tears in my eyes. These were certainly not tears of regret, but tears of emotion that my colleagues, most of them deeply steeped in the long traditions of Inst, and some older than myself, had shown the courage to seize the moment and opt for merit regardless of gender, religion or any other irrelevant consideration. The truth is that Miss Williamson's performance throughout had been quite outstanding. She had behind her, at a relatively young age, five years of experience at Antrim Grammar, and had previously served as deputy head at a boys' school in England.

I did not find it easy, though, to announce the result to the two disappointed candidates. Inevitably they were left with a feeling of "so near and yet so far". I was particularly sorry to give this disappointing news to our own senior Vice Principal, Alan McKinstry, who had sat across the table at so many Board meetings and given wonderful support to Michael Ridley and exemplary service to the school. Our inclusion of Alan in the final interview process indicated our judgement that he would, if chosen, have been a most capable Principal. He continues to play a most important role in the management of our school, to which he has given such outstanding service.

When I called in Janet Williamson to offer her the position, her reaction was a mixture of amazement and exhilaration. When she joined the Governors for a congratulatory drink, only then—with the die already cast—did she say to me: "You know my father." Williamson is a very common name inside and outside Northern Ireland (as in the convenor of the cross-bench peers), and only then did I learn that Janet was the daughter of Maurice Williamson, an old colleague from my civil service days and a dedicated leader of the Boys' Brigade. At once I recalled a happy day in our own lives, when we visited Oxford for the Encaenia at which our daughter Caroline was to graduate. Quite by chance, we had met Maurice Williamson in the town. "What are you doing here, Maurice?" "I am here to see my daughter graduate." "And so am I." So this principal-designate of my old school had been a contemporary of my daughter at Oxford, although they had never met. How small, at times, the world can be! Now she has been in position for more than a year, at a very challenging time for our school and others like it because of the real threat to our essential ethos. With our bicentenary in 2010 ever closer, we are fighting hard to defend what our forefathers created. We are a self-reliant community, and have been willing to bear the heavy burden of our own self-funded capital development to preserve that degree of independence which we think appropriate in a voluntary school. It was a good omen for a new principal when Inst won in her first year the Ulster Schools Cup for rugby football, the trophy for one of the oldest rugby competitions in the world. Few schools can point to two old boys who captained the British Lions. We take pride in an enormous range of extra-curricular activity alongside academic success.

Another chapter in the history of the school ended with a wonderful dinner at Christ Church, meticulously organised by Elizabeth to thank Michael Ridley and his wife Jennie for magnificent service to Inst.

***

My views on the question of academic selection had inevitably been influenced by my exposure to developments in higher education. Shortly after my retirement in 1991 I had been invited to accept appointment as a Crown nominee to the Senate of Queen's University, Belfast. Although I had opted years before to take up a place at Oxford rather than accepting an Open Scholarship to Queen's, I had real affection and respect for this institution which had been so central to the educational and cultural life of my native city. I had known—sometimes well and sometimes more remotely—successive Vice Chancellors since Sir

Eric (later Lord) Ashby. They had conferred upon me, in 1991, the Honorary Degree of Doctor of Laws. As on all such occasions, the conferment of the Honorary Degree had preceded the presentation of regular degrees to students in the particular faculties featuring in the ceremonies that day. Interminable ranks of graduands mounted the stage of the Whitla Hall, the venue for these occasions, in orderly academic ranks and in the order of their degree classification; the proud winners of First Class Honours succeeded by the 2.1s and what were known in my daughter's time at Oxford as "Desmonds" or 2.2s. At last the final student to graduate that day, and by definition well down the academic pecking order, mounted the stage. In a fairly scruffy age, he did not convey an urbane or sophisticated image. Suddenly, before approaching the Vice Chancellor, he veered off towards the microphone put in place for the scheduled speakers, including the Vice Chancellor and the Honorary Graduate. Out of the corner of my eye I could see the Vice Chancellor, Sir Gordon Beveridge, stiffen with apprehension. His tenure of the office had not been an easy time. Issues such as the acceptability of playing the National Anthem had generated more heat than light in student and faculty circles. I could guess that the Vice Chancellor feared some defiant cry of "Tiocfaidh ár lá" (the republican cry of "Our day will come") or other belligerent and divisive message. What actually happened was that this tail-ender took the opportunity to say: "On behalf of all of us, I wanted to say thank you for giving us such a memorable day." A heavy cloud lifted from the concerned head of the Vice Chancellor.

It was also the case that we at Inst regarded Queen's as the lineal successor to our Institution's earlier services to higher education in the North of Ireland. Not only had RBAI provided the only third-level education there before the establishment of the Queen's Colleges at Belfast and elsewhere, but many of the founding fathers of the Queen's College (later the University) had an Instonian background.

I was, therefore, very pleased and honoured to join the Senate, and would have expected to serve there for a good many years but for other developments to which I shall turn in a moment. I was, though, a Senator of the university long enough to identify what I felt to be some weaknesses in the then role and function of the Senate. I could detect, at times, an unhealthy development of factions echoing events outside the university. Some members, it seemed to me, were inclined to view issues not on their merits but through the lens of their ideological commitments. Secondly, I felt that this supposed summit of university governance, normally chaired by the senior Pro-Chancellor, was on too many occasions reactive rather than proactive. Much of its business came upwards to it through the Academic Council and the university's officers, paid and unpaid. At the time of Gordon Beveridge's arrival, there had been some real concern about the financial strength of the institution. They did well for themselves in appointing as Treasurer Sir Ewart Bell, my immediate predecessor as Head of the Northern Ireland Civil Service, a former Permanent Secretary at the Department of Finance, and a person of immense rectitude and thoroughness. In "retirement" these great qualities were made available not only to the university but to the game of rugby football, which he had played as an Irish international, and later, as an administrator at world level, was to be responsible for the World Cup in South Africa, and stood beside Nelson Mandela as he presented the trophy to the Springbok captain, François Pienaar. Ewart would present accounts, financial statements and monitoring data to us in such detail and with such thoroughness that his appeal for comments or questions would often be greeted by a blank silence. On one occasion, I remember, he chided us for our apparent apathy much—I imagine—in the fashion of his late father, an eminent Presbyterian divine. Ewart himself, I often thought, would have made a splendid Moderator.

Too often, though, I felt that we were "blinded with science";

or for that matter, with other arcane domestic mysteries of the university. What I missed was any sense of continuing strategic debate as to how the university could best serve a society in which it played such a central role.

By this time, Queen's had ceased to be the only provider of higher education in the province. As a result of the Lockwood Report, a New University of Ulster had been established at Coleraine, to the great discontent of the people of Derry, who felt that any new university should be sited in the second city and developed around the existing Magee College. I had drafted for Terence O'Neill as Prime Minister a speech for the opening ceremony at Coleraine, and had come to know well the first Vice Chancellor, Dr Alan Burges, and his principal administrative lieutenant, Willie Ewing, an Instonian with a distinguished academic record from Trinity College, Dublin.

Northern Ireland had also been endowed, like other areas of the United Kingdom, with a "polytechnic". Under the charismatic leadership of Derek Birley this had flourished like the green bay tree, while NUU had never quite "cut the mustard". From this, as a consequence of yet another government report, was to flow the merger of the Poly and NUU to form a multi-campus University of Ulster, with sites in Coleraine, at Magee in Londonderry, at Jordanstown on the outskirts of Belfast, and in the old Art College close to St Anne's Cathedral.

The charter of the University of Ulster had included an unusual requirement that, once every seven years, a team from outside the university should consider objectively, and if need be critically, how well it was serving its stated purposes. After all, the merger of a university with a poly was unique. I was asked to participate in such a review, chaired by the eminent Cambridge academic Sir Peter Swinnerton-Dyer, and in our report we emphasized the continuing need for the merged institution to maintain and reinforce those close links with the local society and economy which had characterised the former Ulster Polytechnic.

The merger in Northern Ireland anticipated the shape of things to come at national level. At a stroke the "binary line" was abolished and all over the UK former polytechnics became universities overnight. Some were content to retain an existing local or regional designation; others sought a name which would clothe them with an aura of spurious antiquity, often contrasting with premises from an era of architectural brutalism. So from now on the UK would boast more than a hundred universities— Oxbridge, the ancient foundations of Scotland, the great "civics" and the erstwhile polytechnics. Clearly there would never be enough funding to support all of these as front-rank research institutions as well as centres of degree-level teaching.

Northern Ireland also benefited from one of the few enduring legacies from the Harold Wilson era of gannex raincoats and demonstrative pipe-smoking (for in the privacy of Chequers or Number 10 Wilson preferred a cigar). This was the Open University, and over the years I would grow to appreciate more and more its invaluable role in enabling people to reinforce their professional qualifications, or enjoy learning experiences withheld from them "first time round", on the basis of part-time study. As a BBC Governor I had visited Milton Keynes and been entertained by the engaging Vice Chancellor, Sir John Daniel, but the original idea of relying heavily on broadcast services was being overtaken by other means of communication with students.

For many years, the University Grants Committee had played the key role in distributing government funding to universities in Great Britain, and although their formal writ did not run in Northern Ireland, government there had been guided and advised by a sub-committee of the UGC.

With the abolition of the "binary line", and with the prospect of devolution hanging in the air, it was deemed politic to establish a Higher Education Funding Council for England (HEFCE) and "sister" bodies for Scotland and for Wales. In each of these jurisdictions, universities would find themselves dealing with bodies "at arm's length" from government, albeit constrained by the level of funds made available to them for distribution and the broad policy directions of government.

Northern Ireland presented a special problem in this new environment. It would be difficult to justify setting up a fully independent quango to deal with only two institutions (since the Open University would remain centrally funded). The Funding Councils in Great Britain were made up of a mix of academic and non-academic members. But it could be argued that two represented the worst possible number when it came to funding decisions. Within a set budget, the more funding allocated to Queen's, the less to UU, and vice versa.

The Conservative government of the day therefore decided to establish, not a full Funding Council comparable with those in Great Britain, but an advisory Northern Ireland Higher Council (NIHEC), and I was invited by the minister responsible for our Department of Education, Michael Ancram, to serve as its first chairman. My colleagues would be academic members from outside Northern Ireland and non-academic members from within it, and we would have the benefit of assessors from relevant government departments, and in particular the Department of Education. On acceptance of Michael Ancram's offer, I tendered with real regret my resignation from the Queen's University Senate. Clearly I could not play a role as arbiter between inevitably competing claims, if involved in the governance of one of the claimants.

I would serve as Chairman of NIHEC from 1992 to 2001, reporting both to Conservative and Labour ministers, and to Sean Farren as a local minister during the all-too-brief life of that devolved Executive.

One of the frustrations of operating on an advisory rather than an executive basis is that much of what one does is invisible to a wider public, and indeed to the interests most directly affected. Even now, when we have a Freedom of Information Act and an avowed policy of "open government", ministers remain coy about the release of any material classifiable as advice to them. Yet I was often to compare our profile with that of the long-established Northern Ireland Economic Council. Albeit itself an advisory body, it had not been inhibited from producing reports challenging government, while recognising the prerogative of ministers to reject its advice. Save in this respect, I did not find that the distinction between a full Funding Council and our advisory Council made a great deal of practical difference. While Peter Holmes, the department's senior assessor, gave us useful advice and guidance, we were free to make our own recommendations, and on the whole the department accepted them. We would not have retained the participation of busy and distinguished people for long if they had found their involvement a waste of time. Nevertheless, it could be frustrating to see some other group receiving credit for advice we had given well before.

The main components of the university funding package were the teaching (T) and research (R) elements. Teaching moneys were distributed nationwide on a formulaic basis, recognising the higher costs of certain disciplines, and we could see no sound argument for deviating from the national norm. In any case, many of our students were attending a diversity of universities in Great Britain. The research situation was more complex. Much progress in economic development is research-led and research-driven. In Great Britain some of this research would take place in a university environment, often enabling the university itself to "spin off" innovatory techniques, processes and products into industrial enterprises in which it retained a stake; but there was also a significant research effort in the private sector. By comparison, Northern Ireland, with an economy of small and medium-sized enterprises, had a rather modest capacity to undertake research in the private sector. From the point of view of a local business, availability rather than proximity was the key factor. There was no reason why a firm in Belfast or Londonderry could not exploit and build upon research conducted in Manchester or Nottingham, or for that matter in Galway or Limerick. Nevertheless, the close proximity of industry and research-capability offered the opportunity for beneficial synergy.

It was, perhaps, just about possible that government could have funded relatively wide-ranging research programmes in universities as defined before abolition of the "binary divide". It was inconceivable that this could be afforded across a national range of over a hundred institutions. Government and the Funding Councils were therefore driven towards an ever-increasing emphasis on quality. This quality would be judged in successive Research Assessment Exercises (RAEs) by peer review of the quantity and quality of published research papers in defined areas of assessment. On the basis of this review, the unit of assessment would be given a numerical grading from 5* (work of high international quality) downwards. This would mean that, while a world-class university like Oxford or Cambridge or Imperial College might win high ratings and consequential high levels of R funding, more modest institutions might be obliged to concentrate on achieving decent standards across a relatively concentrated field of activity. Here, though, the small scale of Northern Ireland and its physical isolation from the rest of the United Kingdom were relevant factors. Even in Scotland, though no single university could hope to afford a centre of research excellence in every important discipline, one could more confidently look for this across the whole Scottish higher education system.

We saw it as important to continue to assess Northern Ireland universities according to the "common currency" of the RAE. This would ensure that Queen's and UU could be given reliable ratings on the wider stock-exchange of British higher education. However, we felt there was a "regional factor" related to the comparative isolation of Northern Ireland, which could make a case against the premature reduction or abandonment of support for activities vital to the local economy and society.

Above all, we wanted more units of assessment in Northern Ireland to achieve high RAE ratings on merit because this would open access to other funding streams via the various national Research Councils and the private sector. Our analysis showed, not very surprisingly, that university departments achieving high ratings normally had a very substantial mass of manoeuvre, resulting from investment in buildings and equipment and the attraction of the best available talent in the academic marketplace. For too many years, Northern Ireland's reputation for violence and disorder must have been a disincentive to footloose academics seeking wider opportunities.

A good deal of our time was occupied in preparing evidence for the national inquiry into higher education chaired by Sir Ron (later Lord) Dearing; and we were fortunate indeed that one of his colleagues was Sir George Quigley, who was the principal author of that part of the ultimate report dealing specifically with Northern Ireland. We took real encouragement from Dearing's emphasis on the regional impact of local universities, although we were conscious that many important regions in England could look to a considerable number of institutions within easy reach.

Without further effort and investment, the Northern Ireland universities would find it difficult to maintain their position in the RAE league, let alone improve upon it. At each successive RAE the standards required to achieve the highest ratings rose steadily, and an increasing proportion of the available funding was shifted from the support of mediocrity to the encouragement of excellence. It was therefore a godsend to be told by the Department that an anonymous American donor, now known to be the remarkable Chuck Feeney, would be prepared to contribute £20 million to a Special Programme of University Research, if government would make available a matching £20 million. This had now been agreed, and the money would be allocated as between our two universities following assessment of competitive bids by a panel of academic experts to be drawn from Great Britain and further afield. The task of NIHEC would be to recruit such a panel, and my personal role would be to act as its non-voting chairman. I had expected the recruitment part of the process to be time-consuming and frustrating, as we approached potential candidates in Great Britain, Europe and the USA. I feared that many of those who could spare the time (a whole weekend in Northern Ireland after reading the voluminous bid material) might not be willing to come, while many of those willing to come could not spare the time. To my enormous pleasure, I discovered a real enthusiasm to be involved, and our only withdrawal of a first choice was for health reasons. One had a sense of worldwide academic solidarity.

The disciplines represented on the panel were diverse, but some of the bids were inevitably unrelated to the specific discipline of any individual panel member. They were, however, people well used to making priority judgements within their own institutions, and represented a kind of ad hoc University Grants Committee. The broad range of academic study was well illustrated when our German colleague told me he had come directly from his Research Station in Southern Italy. "And what is your particular field, Professor?" I asked. "The neurological characteristics of crustaceans." The answer summoned up to my memory an entry during my school days in a part of the school magazine which reported the degree-winning achievements of old pupils, and where these had been gained by thesis, gave the title of the thesis itself. So I learned that some scholarly Instonian had won a doctorate by his thesis on "Non-homogeneous lattices in the same plane." I must say the Honorary Doctorate is a much simpler route!

The panel gelled well, the two Vice Chancellors (Sir George Bain from Queen's and Professor Gerry McKenna from UU) made preliminary presentations, and then we went into purdah to weigh the merits of the competing bids. Although the larger slice of funding was allocated to Queen's, the University of Ulster won support for the costliest single project, a new Centre for Biomedical Science. One of the Queen's projects won support by its novelty and intriguing character, marrying music and the sonic arts to trail-blazing scientific research.

I have referred to the participation of the Vice Chancellors of the day. During my time at NIHEC I dealt frequently with them and their predecessors, Sir Gordon Beveridge at Queen's and Sir Trevor Smith (now Lord Smith of Clifton) at UU. While it would have been physically impossible for the chairman or chief executive of HEFCE to maintain close and regular personal contact with all their numerous client institutions, in our case this was both possible because of the scale, and highly desirable because of the absence of local academic members on NIHEC itself. My interlocutors were four very different personalities: Beveridge occasionally oppressed by criticism of employment practices, and perhaps too inclined to clutch to himself problems capable of being handled by senior colleagues; Smith quick, sharp and sometimes abrasive, even when we were available as advocates rather than prosecutors; Bain authoritative and businesslike to a degree; McKenna pleasant, agreeable and well-informed in all his dealings with us, and showing no trace of the problems which later overcame him.

I would also meet, several times a year, the chairmen and chief executives of the three "mainland" Funding Councils. I welcomed these contacts, not least because we had insufficient local university places to satisfy the local demand for higher education, with many thousands over the years—particularly while the "Troubles" persisted—leaving Northern Ireland to study and, too often, meeting a marriage partner "over there" or, sensing better employment opportunities, not returning. This "student emigration" was particularly marked amongst the Protestant population, and a special sense of affinity attracted many of them to Scottish universities. I thought it desirable, in spite of separate Education Departments and separate funding or advisory councils, to keep before us a vision of a wider and interdependent UK higher education system. Later on, devolution would give rise to a more "selfish" attitude to the use of local provision.

A particular area of interest to NIHEC was related to issues of access, participation and student migration. We appointed a special sub-group to examine these issues, chaired by one of our colleagues, Declan Morgan QC, later a High Court Judge. The work of two local academics, Cormack and Osborne, greatly assisted us in pinning down the key facts. With a thrust of government policy not merely to increase the cohort entering higher education but to improve the participation of young people from relatively underprivileged backgrounds, we were gratified to find that we in Northern Ireland were leading the several jurisdictions of the United Kingdom in moving towards these objectives. Participation rates were high, in spite of severe competition for places within the permitted "capped" total admissions, which made it necessary for Queen's in particular to set high entrance standards as represented by "A level points". The University of Ulster could point with justifiable pride to its record in promoting alternative routes to entry, and in effective co-operation with Further Education Colleges.

Student migration was a more complex issue. Not all the students moving to Great Britain did so because they could not gain a place closer to home. They might choose to experience a different (and in dangerous times, more relaxed) atmosphere, or wish to pursue courses or course combinations not available in either of the two local universities. "High flyers" could be attracted by the reputation and cachet of Oxbridge or other institutions in the prestigious "Russell group", to which Queen's has only recently been admitted. We were concerned, though, about a particular group; those from relatively deprived backgrounds who had achieved adequate but not outstanding academic results in adverse circumstances, and for whom the inability to continue study while living at home could present an invidious choice between accepting additional travel or other expense, or abandoning aspirations to a university career.

We believed that, in the ideal university environment, students close to home would benefit from contact with outsiders. Financial pressures, however, could create a situation more like that in parts of the USA, with "State colleges" serving a limited local catchment. Northern Ireland students could encounter the benefits of mixing by moving to Great Britain; those who remained at home would study in more homogeneous communities, unless and until stable and peaceful conditions persuaded more people from outside Northern Ireland to consider on their merits the benefits and attractions of our two universities.

We could see, as a Council, a strong argument for more places. In each of England, Scotland and Wales, the number of university places available was broadly in line with the number of local students seeking higher education, although in each jurisdiction some of those available places would be taken up by students from the other two, from Northern Ireland, or from abroad. In Northern Ireland alone the demand for higher education places substantially exceeded the local supply.

Of course, from the point of view of those administering local expenditure, it could be an attraction to limit our financial liability to student support, rather than the capital and support costs of making more local places available. If a decision were to be reached to remove the "cap" on numbers and provide more places, the options would include the addition of a third university, extensions to and/or better use of the facilities currently existing, and wider exploitation of the distinctly under-used facilities at Stranmillis, previously confined to teacher training.

This was the situation into which the University of Ulster introduced what became known as the "Springvale project". The idea was that the University, in collaboration with the Belfast Institute for Further and Higher Education, would establish a new campus at Springvale, in the heart of a sensitive area of West Belfast. We at NIHEC were not surprised to be asked for our opinion of this concept, and after most careful consideration we advised that, if the primary objective was to provide more higher education, this did not seem to be the most cost-effective way of doing so; but we could understand that there were wider considerations here, including the social, economic and political benefits of regeneration in this sensitive area of Belfast, which must be a matter for judgment by others.

For entirely understandable reasons, the government blessed the concept in broad principle, and while detailed plans to make it a reality were still under discussion, President Bill Clinton visited the site and gave it his blessing. It was most unfortunate, then, that the project would prove to be undeliverable down the line, and I could not help reflecting upon the adverse effects of raising hopes in such an area only to see them ultimately dashed, through earlier failed projects such as the Strathearn Audio or the calamitous De Lorean car project. Better to give root to a healthy plant than to grasp at straws.

4

Culture and the Arts

ALTHOUGH MY OLD SCHOOL HAD IN my time a deserved reputation for the performance of Shakespearean plays, with boys playing the female parts as they would have done in Shakespeare's own day, my sole appearance on the Inst stage was to be in the far from stretching role of the First Officer in *Twelfth Night*, although even my few lines had a fine ring to them: "Orsino, this is that Antonio that took the Phoenix and her fraught from Kandy. And this is he that did the *Tiger* board when your young nephew, Titus, lost his leg. Here in the streets, desperate of shame and state, in private brabble we did apprehend him."

At Oxford, though, I joined a flourishing college dramatic society, the Fantasticks, and won from the most flamboyant and theatrical member of the college the encomium: "A cameo, Kenneth, a cameo."

On my return to Belfast in 1952, I became more and more caught in the "am dram" scene. Membership of the Belfast Drama Circle afforded an opportunity to act in occasional plays and to take part in much more regular play-readings. These we would perform to modest audiences on the top floor of a dilapidated building on High Street, a fire trap to end all fire traps. In the event of disaster, the only exit would have been by parachute and that at too low a level to be effective. For Instonians Dramatic Society (catering for former pupils of RBAI) I acted in Andre Obey's *Noah* and in the wonderful *Juno and the Paycock*. Then, fatefully, I came to the notice of Mary O'Malley. Vivacious, rather beautiful in a dark-eyed Irish way, and peculiarly persistent and persuasive, Mary had gathered together a company, called the Lyric Players, to perform on the stage of a miniscule theatre at the rear of the family home on Belfast's Derryvolgie Avenue. If her physical resources were small, her ambitions were great. First-rate artistic talents, like those of Terence Flanagan the painter or Rowel Friers the cartoonist, were cozened into designing and producing programmes and sets. There were some fine actors and actresses; Sheelagh Garvin (later to be Flanagan's wife), Denis Tuohy (a future television announcer), Norman Stevenson (a master at Inst with a slight build but a beautiful speaking voice), and a senior Civil Service colleague in Arthur Brooke, of whom no more need be said than that he performed a most memorable Oedipus. Mary was demanding to work for, and after each appearance on her stage I would say to myself, "No more!" Now, though, I see what a privilege it was to play Horatio in Mary's *Hamlet*, or form part of a modern-day Greek chorus in TS Eliot's *Family Reunion*, although I hated the play at the time. Mary herself was a fervent Irish nationalist, both culturally and politically. For her, Shakespeare or Eliot would always take second place to WB Yeats. It was, then, all the odder that so many of her actors were not only loyal members of the Northern Ireland Civil Service but also, like Arthur Brooke or Ron Jones, Englishmen.

From this tiny but exotic bud there grew in time the professional Lyric Theatre, which gave early exposure to the talents of such as Liam Neeson. The ultimate control rested until recently with the members of the Lyric Association, of whom I was one, who held the shares and elected the members of the

[114]

governing Board. As I write, work is about to begin to replace the present theatre, with its adequate auditorium but grossly inadequate back-stage accommodation, with a modern and fit-for-purpose building. The Arts Council and Belfast City Council will meet a substantial part of the cost, and a massive fund-raising exercise, led by Sir George Bain, has met with heartening support and success. On 20 January 2008 Elizabeth and I visited the old theatre for the last event before reconstruction, a wonderful evening of anecdote and reminiscence.

If I had come early to theatre, I came comparatively late to opera. I was well into middle-age when, finding myself with a free evening in London, I passed close to Covent Garden and saw the playbills for Mussorgsky's *Boris Godunov*. Because I needed only a single ticket, I was able to join an enthralled audience held enraptured by Boris Christoff in the title role. The music was dynamic and the settings exotic to a degree. So it was that, during my time on the BBC Board of Governors, I took advantage of the opportunity to hear at Covent Garden almost every operatic star of the day; Domingo, Pavarotti, Kiri te Kanawa, Angela Georghiu, James Allen and numerous others. I found the Wagnerian *Ring* a little heavy for my taste, and in one controversial production of *Rheingold* the scenery and costumes were so grotesquely awful as to persuade me that I could only enjoy the music with my eyes closed. On the other hand *Meistersinger* was a pure delight from beginning to end. Since those days I have visited opera houses in such places as Budapest, Prague and Hamburg, and I have happy memories of the Wexford Opera Festival, a wonderful cocktail of song and Guinness!

With this background, I was more than happy to accept in 1992 an invitation to join the Board of Opera Northern Ireland. We had many assets during my five years on that Board, not least the services of Bill Montgomery of Greyabbey (a member of one of the oldest "planted" families) as chairman and Stephen Barlow (the conductor husband of the delicious and hilarious

Joanna Lumley) as artistic director. Our policy, inevitable in view of our limited resources, was to engage professional principals to be supported by our amateur chorus. Sometimes the result would be exceptional; I remember, for instance, a *Tosca* every bit as good as some I had seen and heard in far more prestigious places. However, we tended to get our fingers burned in economic terms when seeking to stage operas which, while far from being avant-garde, were just outside the "safe" repertoire of *Tosca*, *Madam Butterfly* or *La Boheme*. We could only exist with substantial Arts Council subsidy, and despite our valiant efforts at outreach, were always vulnerable to criticism as "elitist" art aimed at an affluent minority, in the process diverting money away from more localised and populist activities dispersed around the province. We did what we could, but the inescapable truth of the matter is that opera is a high art, and if it is to achieve a certain standard, an expensive one. Moreover the Grand Opera House in the centre of Belfast, splendid Matcham theatre though it is, could not then offer the space and facilities for an agreeable social evening built around the performance. At Castle Ward the stage is tiny and the auditorium cramped, but the wider venue is able to offer to ordinary members and corporate sponsors a hint of the Glyndebourne experience. Wexford, too, has carved out a special place for itself in the Irish social calendar. Buoyed up on a tide of Guinness or best Irish whiskey, audiences could experience operas seldom performed—albeit often for good reason—and promising young singers on the rise before their engagement costs a king's ransom. Increasingly I wondered whether Ireland as a whole could support more than one domestic professional opera company, available to perform in Dublin, Belfast or elsewhere. Ironically, the Grand Opera House has now been extended and upgraded to create the kind of venue we were crying out for.

After I retired from the Board in 1997, growing concern about funding and finance was to lead eventually to a winding-up of the company. Since then the operatic experience in Belfast has been provided for the most part by touring companies from the former Soviet Union, offering performances of very variable quality.

However, further challenges and opportunities would await me. One of my earliest tasks as a young civil servant in the Fifties had been to act as secretary to a committee established to explore the case for an Ulster Folk Museum. When the recommendation was positive, it later fell to me, as private secretary to the Finance Minister, to work up a case for consideration by the Cabinet, and subsequently to instruct the Draftsman on the heads of legislation to give the new museum a statutory basis. Thereafter I followed with great interest and satisfaction the steady development of the Ulster Folk Museum at Cultra, near Holywood in County Down. This open-air museum, after the pattern of Skansen in Stockholm and St Fagan's near Cardiff, was to prove a great attraction both for local people and visitors to Northern Ireland. Later, with the addition of transport collections accumulated by the old Belfast Museum, the Cultra museum could boast both folkways and transport exhibits, including one of the best railway collections in the country.

For many years much of the transport collection had been kept in storage, and seen by very few. Year by year, as ministers considered what to fit into the last remaining tranche of public expenditure, the desirability of a proper home for the railway collection would be raised, acknowledged and deferred for a further year. At last it came to the final occasion before my retirement when I could contribute to these discussions. In essence I said: "We can't go on forever saying it should be done, but not just now. Do me a favour, and agree to fit it in this time." To my huge pleasure, my importunities were successful, and the railway project received a green light. When the massive building was completed at Cultra, Elizabeth and I were invited to the formal opening ceremony to be performed by Sir Patrick Mayhew as Secretary of State for Northern Ireland. When these honours had been done, Mayhew announced he had another duty to perform. I was led to a simulated railway platform upon which some kind of notice was concealed by a cloth or covering. When I was invited to pull a cord to remove this, what was revealed was a station sign bearing the name "Bloomfield", which had stood on the halt of that name on the abandoned track of the old Belfast and County Down Railway.

Perhaps it is this association which led in time to an invitation to become the Northern Vice President of the Railway Preservation Society of Ireland. My Southern opposite number was (and is) Garret Fitzgerald, a former Taoiseach, while the President is the nephew of my old Prime Ministerial boss, Lord O'Neill of Shane's Castle, a railway buff of the first order. If O'Neill is unavailable, Fitzgerald or I have to chair the AGM of the Society. On the couple of occasions I have done so, business has been transacted without difficulty or controversy. However, I attended one memorable AGM in Dublin, chaired by Garret Fitzgerald, when for some strange reason the spirit of the barrack-room lawyer was in the air, and the proceedings were lengthy and contentious. At their conclusion, Garret confided to me that he had found it rather less stressful to preside, during his presidency of the European Union over meetings of European Prime Ministers. For me, the appointment was a treat; not least when travelling in state from Dublin to Dun Laoghaire in the restored Irish State Coach in the company of the President of Ireland. Only with difficulty did I resist the temptation to bow graciously at the carriage window.

A second jewel in our cultural crown was the Ulster American Folk Park or museum of emigration outside Omagh. Its "true begetter" had been an old civil service colleague of mine, Eric Montgomery. As Director of Information one of his principal duties had been to act as liaison between the Stormont government and the press; and frankly he was not very good at this, because I suspect he did not greatly like the press, or they him. On the other hand, he was a truly creative "ideas man". He had been a strong ally in the cause of establishing a Folk Museum, but his particular passion was for promoting the extraordinary links between Ulster and the USA. He was fascinated that so many American presidents had been the sons of Ulster emigrant families, and at his initiative the family homes in Ulster which survived were identified, marked and publicised. His interest in America was not confined to the curtilage of the White House. Another great and powerful family in the development of the USA had been the Mellons, whose origins lay in a humble farm at Dergalt, near Omagh in County Tyrone. Eric formed a friendship with a scholarly member of the contemporary Mellon generation, Dr Matthew Mellon, and with his financial and other support the homestead was restored and presented to the world at an extraordinary opening ceremony which featured very rich, sophisticated and well-dressed members of the clan gathered in the midst of an Ulster farmyard. That opening had not exhausted Montgomery's ambition. Harvesting government work-support programmes, accumulating little piles of money from here and there, he became the prime mover in establishing in that area of County Tyrone a truly remarkable museum. Here one can visit the sorts of homes occupied by emigrants to the United States, moved from their original locations and restored, and pass through a simulated emigrant ship to view examples—brought from America—of the sort of life those emigrants would have lived there. The Omagh museum now has its "twin" at Staunton in Virginia, featuring homes from Ulster and the other areas from which immigrants travelled to that part of the United States.

My work on the Folk Museum project had often brought me into contact with the then Director of the Belfast Museum at Stranmillis, WA Seaby, and strangely his young son had also been a member of the Lyric Players company. This Belfast Museum became the national museum of Northern Ireland, and the original rather elegant building had been greatly extended by a pretty brutal example of modern architecture which many architectural buffs greatly admire. I had known this museum since childhood, been fascinated—like so many other children—by its

Egyptian mummy, and rejoiced in its enrichment by the "Gerona" treasure, a wonderful collection of artefacts recovered from the sea-bed off the North Antrim coast from a Spanish Armada shipwreck by the Belgian marine archeologist, Robert Stenuit.

With this background, I was greatly intrigued by advertisements appearing in local newspapers in 2002, inviting applications to serve as chairperson or member of the National Museums and Galleries of Northern Ireland, an organisation established some years before to control and merge in the national interest the cultural assets represented by the Folk and Transport Museum, the Ulster American Folk Park and the Ulster Museum in Belfast with its offshoot, the Armagh County Museum in the cathedral and primatial city, the ecclesiastical capital of Ireland. I applied to be considered both for the chair and for ordinary membership of the Board, but would not have applied for the chair if I had appreciated that Margaret Elliott, the very efficient incumbent and founding chair, was eligible for and interested in a further term. The appointing department did well to reappoint Margaret, and I was more than happy to accept appointment as a Board member and serve under her. I was honoured to be asked to serve as the Vice Chairman, to act as chair of the important Audit Committee and to become one of the directors of W5, Northern Ireland's science centre, established as an important element of our principal millenium project, the Odyssey complex on the dockside. W5 was a separate company, but under the ultimate control of MAGNI, and we were enormously fortunate to have available as our chairman the calm and imperturbable Dan Harvey, an experienced banker, and as our chief executive, the enthusiastic and creative Sally Montgomery.

From the start I intended to serve only a single term. At its completion I would be seventy-five, and I did not think it sensible to soldier on until nearly eighty, even if the appointing department were prepared to allow me to do so. I found MAGNI facing a challenge all too familiar to me. When several organisations are brought together in a new body, the fusion is not something achieved overnight. The task of the new umbrella body would be to create and foster a more coherent, united and effective structure to manage and develop the several sites. As chairman of the Audit Committee I was bound to be concerned about qualification of our accounts by our auditors, but it was clear to all of us that proper structure at the top level of management would be required to give real focus to the organisation. The Ulster Museum was ageing and unable to exploit adequately its advantages as a primary visitor attraction, while W5—like other science centres across the United Kingdom—could not hope to be totally self-supporting. Some of the necessary support would come from government, but we also looked to the Odyssey Trust to play its part. The attractions had to be regularly updated and renewed, and cash stringency placed heavy burdens on Sally Montgomery and her staff. The arrival on the scene of a new chief executive, Tim Cooke, whose previous career had been at the BBC, brought a new sense of urgency, and patient negotiation won the great prize of capital funding for the modernisation of the Ulster Museum, inevitably involving its temporary closure while the works are carried out.

Of course no museum can hope to remain indefinitely attractive on the basis of its permanent collections alone, and I could see for myself what a boost travelling or temporary exhibitions of high standard could give. As an historian, I valued in particular a wonderful exhibition of documents and artefacts relating to the Act of Union, while an earlier role as Victims Commissioner qualified me to make some direct input into a most moving "Conflict" exhibition. Each year there would be great interest in an annual exhibition, sponsored by W & G Baird, based on pictures by a chosen artist with local associations, some of which would be reproduced in a series of calendars which would become in time museum pieces in their own right.

As my term on the Board of MAGNI came to its end in June

2006, I felt we had made real progress in establishing a robust structure and recruiting able staff to fill key positions. We could look forward to substantial capital investment in the improvement of our facilities. Even a PAC report critical of some of our storage facilities had been more helpful than not, since we were well aware of the deficiencies they identified, and more than willing to tackle them, if given the necessary resources to do so. On the revenue side, however, the outlook was less promising. Through better shopping and catering facilities we could hope to step up our revenue-earning activities. Yet even on the most optimistic projections on the revenue side, we could foresee increasing difficulty in maintaining our three sites (with the Armagh Museum then expected to pass to local government in the impending reorganisation of public bodies). A renewed Board would have formidable challenges to face, and the outcome would be crucial to the cultural health and well-being of Northern Ireland.

Another element in my little cultural "portfolio" had been membership of the Management Committee of the Armagh Observatory and Planetarium. The ultimate responsibility for the Observatory, founded by Archbishop Robinson of Armagh in the eighteenth century, rested with a Board of Governors, chaired ex officio by the Primate of the day, and consisting of the Dean and Chapter of Armagh with a limited number of others. In more recent times the Board had in practice devolved the effective responsibility for the ongoing administration. This, too, would be chaired by the Archbishop, but would bring into play, alongside members appointed or co-opted by the Governors, others nominated by the funding department in government, Queen's University, the Particle Physics and Astronomy Research Council, and the Dublin Institute of Advanced Studies.

The Observatory itself dated back to 1790, and its buildings from that period included one of the earliest astronomical domes to survive in the world, accompanying a unique collection of instruments of historical importance. Robinson had an ambition to move forward from his Observatory to the creation of a university at Armagh, and it is ironic that a couple of hundred years were to pass before Queen's University, with its then Pro-Vice Chancellor Mary McAleese in the lead, took steps to establish an "outreach centre" in the city, which unfortunately did not flourish as hoped and expected.

The Planetarium, at that time only the second in the United Kingdom, had been added in 1968, and the early association with the eccentric but universally known Patrick Moore had raised its early profile.

I myself had first heard of the Observatory in the late Fifties, while serving as private secretary to the Minister of Finance. Since, in those days, government funding had come from that department, the Minister of the day, Brian Maginess, decided to pay a visit and was shown round by the then current director, Dr Eric Lindsay, who had greatly advanced the interests of the Observatory, both by forming a consortium with Harvard and Dunsink in the South and by attracting one of the leading astrophysicists of the day, the Estonian émigré Ernest Opik. During the visit, it seems, Dr Opik had burst in upon the director, crying excitedly: "Dr Lindsay, Dr Lindsay, the Portadown Chamber of Commerce is demanding to see the moon, and there is no moon!" Today the great Estonian's grandson, Lembit Opik, is a Liberal Democrat Member of Parliament, and includes in his idiosyncratic portfolio of interests a concern about possible collisions with near-earth objects. An old boy of RBAI, he is, I would suppose, the only person who can claim to be both Instonian and Estonian. He could be said to make a unique contribution to British public life and our relations with Eastern Europe.

By the time I arrived on the scene, the Observatory was coping valiantly with two disabilities. First, its complement of mature astronomers was relatively small, making the achievement of a 4 rating in the RAE, in competition with large university departments, all the more creditable. Secondly, it had to be recognised that Northern Ireland, with its clouded skies, light pollution at night and other drawbacks, was not the ideal place for direct astronomical observation. Instead, Armagh had to be a centre for interpretation of pictures and other data transmitted from elsewhere, and this was recognised by the decision to be one of the international participants in the project for a South African Large Telescope (SALT). Nevertheless on each visit to the Observatory for a meeting of the Management Committee or one of its sub-groups, I would be impressed to meet young people from many distant countries who had come to undertake research there. Wisely the director, Professor Mark Bailey, had decided to concentrate effort on well-defined fields such as solar physics, solar-terrestrial connections and climatologic, star formation and near-earth impact hazards

A further profound challenge was presented to the Governors and Management Committee when, for health and safety reasons, it was necessary to close the Planetarium for a prolonged period. Its director, Dr Tom Mason, set himself the task of persuading government to provide funding, not just for remedial works and reconstruction, but for modernisation and upgrading of the whole Planetarium experience. He was also determined to use the period of closure not to go into institutional hibernation but to enhance the outreach programme, particularly to schools. I always saw both the Planetarium and W5 as key instruments in the vital regional and national task of enhancing the interest of young people in science and technology.

However, we could by no means assume that adequate funding would continue to be available without making a strong and continuing case for the institution as a unique cultural, scientific and educational asset. Those of us who were not scientists, let alone astronomers, began to feel that even the Management Committee could not offer all the necessary support and advice to the two directors. With two of my colleagues, Professor Merrifield and Aine Downey, I worked up "options for the future" which called for the establishment of new Research and Education sub-committees, each capable of offering a sharper and more professional focus. These Committees would not control or manage the directors, but advise, encourage and support them. The Research Committee is now in being. As my term of office came to an end in 2006, I had every hope that the Armagh Observatory and Planetarium would continue their scientific and educational work into the third century of Primate Robinson's foundation, but it remains to be seen whether the rate of funding will make this possible.

5

Bishops for a New Century

Sir Kenneth and Lady Bloomfield

Major George Pilkington, Divisional Commander, The Salvation Army, Sir James Galway, flautist, Lady Bloomfield, Chairman of the Advisory Board of The Salvation Army, and an accompanist

Lady Bloomfield presents a copy of *We Will Remember Them* to Hillary Clinton. John Hume's wife Pat looks on

Sir Kenneth and Lady Bloomfield at the Pentagon with John Warner, Secretary of the US Navy

An "Ian Gow" event at Hillsborough Castle with the Peter Brookes, Brian Mawhinney, Jane Gow and a recipient

Mr. Peter McLachlan, Director of Bryson House and Lady Bloomfield meet Diana, Princess of Wales

Sir Patrick Mayhew, the Secretary of State for Northern Ireland, asks Sir Kenneth to unveil the sign for the old "Bloomfield" station at the opening of Cultra's railway collection

Sir Kenneth receives the Northern Ireland Chamber of Commerce Trophy for Excellence at the Culloden Hotel

Sir Kenneth at a London dinner with Lord Sterling of P and O and Sir John Parker

With Jacques Santer, then President of the European Commission

Lady Bloomfield at a fundraising event with Lady Mayhew; Pat Killen presenting a Tyrone crystal microphone to broadcaster Sue McGregor

Sir Kenneth with Lord Rana at an Indian community event

Members of the Review Group on the Constitution of Jersey

Lady Bloomfield and Dame Jane Gow with the trustees of the Ian Gow Memorial Fund on a visit to Northern Ireland

The late John Wilson and Sir Kenneth present an award to Senator George Mitchell in the presence of Dermot Ahern

A visit to the Commonwealth War Graves Cemetery in Comilla, Bangladesh

Lady Bloomfield receives a clock to mark the end of her eight year term as chairman of the Advisory Committee of The Salvation Army

Pianist Barry Douglas receives a Tyrone Crystal piano from Lady Bloomfield during an " Ian Gow" fundraising concert at Hillsborough Castle

Sir Kenneth meets the Queen at Windsor Castle

At a British-Irish Association conference with Sir John Chilcot of the Northern Ireland Office and Len Appleyard, later Ambassador to China

Lady Bloomfield at Hazelwood Integrated College for the Ian Gow
Memorial Fund

With President Mary McAleese and her husband Martin at Aras an
Uachtarain

Lady Bloomfield visits the library at Hazelwood College donated from Ian Gow funds

Eamonn Holmes supporting The Salvation Army Christmas Appeal

Sir Kenneth and Lady Bloomfield escort victims to a meeting with Prince Charles at Highgrove

Lady Bloomfield, their son Timothy and daughter Caroline with Sir Kenneth as he receives an Honorary Doctorate at Queen's University, Belfast

IN WRITING OF THE NORTHERN IRELAND Higher Education Council, I have explained that during my term as its first chairman, all the academic members were drawn from Great Britain. One of these was Pauline Perry, a tiny, vivacious and ferociously able woman who had become Vice Chancellor of South Bank University in London, one of the former polytechnics receiving that status after abolition of the "binary divide". Created a Life Peeress in 1991 (as Baroness Perry of Southwark), she proved a formidable member of our Council, and it was a matter of great regret to me when, in 1994, the pressure of other (and multiple) commitments forced her to withdraw from our work.

Quite out of the blue, Pauline telephoned me at home one evening in early 1999. She explained that one of her many roles was membership of the General Synod of the Church of England. There had been a growing view within the Church that the rather arcane processes leading ultimately to the appointment of diocesan bishops should be revisited and re-examined. As a consequence the Synod had decided to invite a committee to consider the role of the Crown Appointments Commission and other relevant matters. Baroness Perry had been chosen to chair this eminent committee, made up of distinguished clerical and lay members of the Church. The Bishop of Rochester would be acting as a theological consultant, but it was envisaged that there would also be a lay consultant, bringing to the discussions background knowledge of appointment procedures outside the Church. For whatever reason, Pauline had identified me as a potential consultant in that capacity. I would not, she was careful to explain, receive any remuneration if I accepted, save for the recoupment of travel and other expenses, and the only reward she could offer was to be involved with a group of fascinating people in a very challenging exercise. I doubt if she could have known how sensitive the question of fair appointment procedures had become in my native place, or to what religious tradition, if any I belonged. I could, for all she knew, have been Roman Catholic or Presbyterian or Jewish. I had, as it happened, been baptised in the Church of England and confirmed in the Anglican Church of Ireland.

Inevitably I had, as a senior civil servant, been involved over many years in the process of identifying people with potential for future advancement, and in the work of selection for promotion in our hierarchy. While I had become a rather irregular attender and communicant, my cultural and spiritual home lay within the Anglican Communion. I had been confirmed in St Donard's Church of Ireland in the Bloomfield area of Belfast (unhappily not a family demesne), as had the Church of England Bishop Williamson, a relative of our new Inst Principal, who had chaired CRAC (the Central Religious Advisory Council), during my time at the BBC. My Oxford experience, too, had steeped me in Anglicanism. The founder of St Peter's Hall had been the famous Bishop Chavasse of Liverpool, the driving force behind the building of that city's great Anglican cathedral, and his son Christopher, first Master of the new college, had been later Bishop of Rochester, one of the most ancient dioceses in the Church. While in no sense a theological college, St Peter's Hall (today St Peter's College) provided an Oxford education for many young men—often from modest backgrounds—who became clergy in the Church of England. OICCU—the Oxford Inter-Collegiate Christian Union—was very active in college and university during my time, but oddly enough I was never approached or proselytised by them. Perhaps, in a largely evangelical college, my appearance on the scene had given rise to suspicion that a crypto-Romanist was in their midst. Any such fear would have been totally groundless, given the general tone of the Church of Ireland.

I was lucky enough to count as a real friend the then Primate of All-Ireland and Archbishop of Armagh, Dr Robin (Lord) Eames. He had proved himself not only to be an outstanding leader of the Church of Ireland in very testing times, but had been regarded by many in the wider communion as a potential Archbishop of Canterbury. At one stage, not least because Margaret Thatcher was known to hold him in high esteem, this had seemed a real possibility. When this translation did not take place, the wider Anglican Communion had not failed to use to the full his background of legal education and his consummate powers of diplomacy in confronting the most difficult and potentially divisive issues, such as the ordination of women and the elevation to higher posts in the Church of avowedly gay clerics. Apart from other encounters, Robin and I would meet from time to time at meetings of the Armagh Observatory Management Committee. When he was asked to cope with the situation arising out of the consecration by the Episcopal Church of the USA of a gay Bishop of New Hampshire, I could not forebear from recalling a wonderful old movie called *Heavens Above*, in which Peter Sellers, playing a Church of England vicar of boundless goodness and naiveté, tried to behave as Christ himself would have done; for example, by housing scruffy and disreputable families in the vicarage of his rather "posh" parish. The consequences had been so disruptive that the PM and Archbishop of Canterbury are seen to put their heads together at the highest level. As a consequence the final scene shows a space rocket heading into the empyrean, while transmitting back to earth the jolly voice of the hymn-singing vicar, who has just been appointed "Bishop of Outer Space". Perhaps, I mischievously suggested, the current problem could be solved by promoting the Bishop of New Hampshire to be the first Archbishop of Outer Space? But in truth it was no laughing matter, either for Archbishop Eames or the wider communion, with the potential for the worldwide fellowship to be torn asunder by the conflict between American "liberalism" and African "traditionalism".

My childhood attendance at church and Sunday School had left me with the most wonderful inheritance of the King James Bible and the Book of Common Prayer. I am, I fear, a traditionalist in these and other matters. I did not go along with the notion that these beautiful and emotive words were now incomprehensible, and that the finest fillet should be replaced by scrag end. I have little doubt that, had I been born a Roman Catholic, I would have become one of the stubborn defenders of the Tridentine Mass.

I liked the idea of being "at home" spiritually even when "abroad" in the general sense. I shall, for instance, never forget attending a service during one of my periodic visits to Washington in that city's great Episcopal cathedral. The sermon, I remember, was preached by the Dean of Oklahoma City, and as he described the consequences of the notorious terrorist outrage there, I related—as an Ulsterman—to so much of what he had to say. I also remember with great vividness the voice of the principal officiating cleric—I would suppose a Dean or canon of the cathedral. This black American had a voice which was like Paul Robeson speaking prose. It was deep, resonant, deliberate and beautifully phrased. If God himself had been an American, He would have sounded like this. I have used the word "deliberate". In my native province, Dr Ian Paisley had been for much of his life a divisive figure, but I have never been in any doubt that his platform oratory gains a great deal from the deliberation with which he speaks. He-gives-every-word-its-full-value.

As well as being raised as an Anglican, my academic training had been as an historian, and I could see at once that the Perry group would be dealing with institutions and procedures deeply rooted in our history. And so I said, "Yes."

We would work for many months, usually at Church House in Westminster. I was fascinated by the participants, the witnesses and the issues. My colleagues included the affable Bishop of Sheffield (Jack Nicholls), the sort of cleric one could envisage happily mixing in a local pub with both believers and non-believers, Nicholas Baines (now Archdeacon of Lambeth), who had taken holy orders after a spell as a Russian specialist at GCHQ, and Dr Philip Giddings, a leading lay member of the Synod. I was particularly fascinated and intrigued by our theological consultant, the Bishop of Rochester, Michael Nazir-Ali. Here, after all, was an immigrant from Pakistan who had not only risen to a very senior position in the episcopacy, but had received recognition as one of the great scholars of the Anglican tradition. We were kept on the straight and narrow by our assessors, Philip Mawer, then Secretary General of the General Synod and later Parliamentary Commissioner for Standards, and Brian Hanson, Legal Advisor to the Archbishops' Council. Above all, I was greatly impressed by our secretary, Dr Colin Podmore. A secretary can be anything from a mere amanuensis to a major influence on the membership, and Colin, fortified by his impressive scholarly knowledge of the Church's affairs, was certainly in the latter category. Pauline Perry's chairmanship was firm, courteous and orderly; hardly a surprise, since she had chaired or served on numberless committees, commissions and inquiries, and was by this time a Head of House at Cambridge, as President of Lucy Cavendish College.

If we had examined an impressive array of witnesses in the Jersey exercise, the array offering evidence to the Perry group was even more impressive, including as it did the Archbishops of Canterbury and York, eight diocesan bishops, other senior figures in the Church, and the Appointments Secretaries to the Archbishops and the Prime Minister.

Inevitably, as our work proceeded, I would compare and contrast the situation vis a vis appointments in the Church with those in the world outside. I identified a real sense of the episcopacy as a calling, and not just a "job". I reflected that part of the ritual for installing a new Speaker of the House of Commons involved a token show of resistance on his part; yet, in reality, it seemed to me that those appointed had been more than willing to seek and obtain the post. What the outside world might regard as a "promotion" in the Church could on occasions seem to the central figure more of a cross to bear. We took evidence, for example, from the current holder of one of the most senior diocesan positions in the Church. When approached, he already held the office of bishop elsewhere, albeit in a position of lesser prominence. His wife and family were most happily settled in their local home and schools. He made it clear to us that he had accepted the translation not with any sense of exhilaration, but rather out of a sense of duty to his calling and under pressure to accept both from his Archbishop and Number 10.

We were not dealing here with businessmen—although the conduct of a diocese in the modern world involves many business issues—but with deeply committed Christians, who held to the belief that, in the designation of people to lead the Church, allowance must be made for the working of the Holy Spirit. Some, at least, seemed to feel it almost indecent to sense a higher calling and to pursue it. Improbably I was reminded at times of the oft-repeated television advertisement for the National Lottery, in which a huge finger reaches down to touch some fortunate individual.

Nevertheless, we were coming to the conclusion that the existing processes were far too secretive and hugger-mugger. We agonised over the question of whether candidates for a diocesan vacancy should be interviewed—as would certainly have been the case for appointments of comparable weight in the world outside, particularly in the public sector—and we were, after all, discussing here the affairs of a "state" or established church. We were not the only European country to preserve such a direct link between state and church. When I had visited Scandinavia to look at their arrangements for public service training, the equivalent of the Permanent Secretary at their Ministry of Administrative Affairs (shades of *Yes, Minister*) had said to me at one stage: "I must show you the room of a lady colleague upstairs. What she does will be of no interest to you, but it has the best view in the whole of Stockholm." The view was, indeed, splendid, but I could not resist asking its occupier: "What exactly do you do in the Department?", and I shall never forget the answer: "I appoint bishops."

The degree of secrecy surrounding the Anglican process had given rise to rather absurd fancies of anonymous Appointments Secretaries sitting in inconspicuous pews at remote churches talent-spotting, like football managers looking for a new striker. We felt the process should be much more open, that a known wish to be considered for advancement did not represent the sin of pride, and that those involved in making recommendations should have access to standardised and reliable information about the people under consideration.

We were not, however, invited or empowered to consider the most controversial of issues. The title Crown Appointments Commission reflected the fact that the Queen remained, as her predecessors had been since Tudor times, the Supreme Governor of the Church of England. Since we lived in an era in which most important functions of the Crown were in practice devolved to Her Majesty's Ministers, the final decision about an episcopal appointment rested with the Prime Minister. After all the earlier sifting, two names, in order of preference, would be recommended to the Prime Minister of the day. He or she could choose either of these, or ask for a further name or names. Yet there was nowadays no guarantee that a Prime Minister would himself be an Anglican, a Protestant, a Christian or a believer in any religion whatever. There remained a religious test to assure the "Protestant succession" to the Throne itself; a similar constraint formerly applying to the office of Lord Chancellor had been removed; we had a current Prime Minister who was married to a Roman Catholic and would convert to Catholicism after retirement; and with all the emphasis on multi-culturalism, how could one rule out the possibility of a future Jewish or Muslim or Hindu Prime Minister? This was entirely possible in principle, if not imminent in practice. There was the further difficulty that no one could know what criteria would weigh most heavily in the mind of any individual Prime Minister as he or she scanned the recommendations coming forward through the established machinery. What was his "churchmanship", evangelical or high-church? Where did he stand in relation to key issues like the ordination of women? Was he, in a socio-political sense, "one of us"? We were not invited to consider, and did not consider such issues. I doubt, however, whether they will go away. Other member churches of the Anglican Communion have found different and perfectly satisfactory ways of regulating their affairs. In the disestablished Church of Ireland, the House of Bishops itself selects a person to fill any diocesan vacancy. Some would consider that the ending of establishment would strengthen rather than weaken the Church of England; others would consider it a gross error and a brutal severance from deeply entrenched tradition.

As our thoughts began to come together, Pauline Perry invited us to an extended meeting in Cambridge at Lucy Cavendish College. Until this visit, I had not appreciated the unique position and history of that college. The name Lucy Cavendish recalls a victim of earlier violence in Ireland than I had witnessed, for she was the widow of Lord Frederick Cavendish, Chief Secretary for Ireland, who had been assassinated by Fenian terrorists in May 1882 in Dublin's Phoenix Park. Thereafter, Lucy Cavendish had taken up the cause of women's education, and in tribute to her, a college established specifically for mature women seeking a Cambridge education had been given her name. It was a happy reminder that male chauvinism is far from universal, since numerous loving husbands have been content to see their wives detached for a time from the cares of home and family to pursue a long-felt ambition. In these peaceful surroundings we were able not only to pursue important issues to a conclusion, but to acknowledge the spiritual underpinning of our work in the college chapel.

So we came, at last, to the stage of finalising our report to the General Synod. Just as I had, as a member of the Law Reform Advisory Committee, felt myself at times to be a generalist amongst focussed experts, so I felt that my role on the Perry group had been confined to some description, as distinct from advocacy, of appointment standards and practices elsewhere. Perhaps my only significant contribution was the last stage of all. To attract public interest, reports have to be given a catchy headline title rather than a prosy precis of the contents. We discussed, and rejected, title after title. I had, however, remembered how often, when describing some lay appointments procedure, I had been reminded that "you are not allowing for the Holy Spirit". So, with some diffidence, I suggested: "Why not call our report *Working with the Spirit*?", and they settled for that.

Our report, when published in 2001, was detailed, considered and constructive, rather than controversially radical. It recommended renaming the Crown Appointments Commission as the Episcopal Nominations Commission and called for more emphasis on seeking potential and evidence of it, not confined to experience as a suffragan bishop or archdeacon, and altogether more transparent and open procedures. A new system should be "fair, thorough, representative and effective". The report incorporated for those of a more scholarly bent a remarkable paper—*Towards a Theology of Choosing Bishops* by Michael Nazir-Ali, and a wide-ranging historical survey by Colin Podmore on

The Choosing of Bishops in the Early Church and in the Church of England. I was glad to have played even a small part in this fascinating exercise, bringing me for a brief period across the line from the profane to the sacred.

6

The Victims of Terrorism

I NOW COME TO MUCH THE most onerous and sensitive task of a "new life".

When Labour came to power in 1997, the new Prime Minister, Tony Blair, made it very clear that dealing with the Northern Ireland problem would rate very high amongst his priorities. His predecessor in office, John Major, had also taken an exemplary interest but had moved very cautiously, taking account of the vulnerable position of his deeply divided party in the House of Commons, and of an underlying feeling that supping with the representatives of militant republicanism called for a very long spoon, and some degree of clarity about their intentions for the "armed struggle".

In his early visits to Northern Ireland as Prime Minister, Blair was vigorously lobbied by a wide range of more or less vociferous interests. Amongst these, representatives of those who had suffered most directly from three decades of violence—widows and other bereaved people, and victims still carrying the physical and emotional scars of violent attacks upon them—made a very powerful impression. There was at that time much talk of amnesty, of the early release of prisoners, of bringing people and communities in from the cold. "What about us?" they asked. "Are we to be the forgotten victims of this conflict?"

Thus the conviction grew at Number 10 Downing Street and in the Northern Ireland Office that something constructive needed to be done about this issue. So it was that, quite out of the blue, I was sounded by one of Mo Mowlam's most senior and experienced officials, John Steele, as to whether I would be prepared to lead a Victims Commission to advise government as to how these sufferings might best be recognised. I asked for a little time to think about this invitation to serve. I saw at once that I would be entering an emotional and political minefield. To begin with, who in truth were "the victims"? In some sense we were all victims, because no one who had lived through thirty years of appalling violence could have avoided some degree of disruption of normal life. Our own children had grown up never knowing a peaceful Northern Ireland. As compared to the easy-going fun of my own life in the late Forties and early Fifties— sweaty animated dances fuelled by nothing more addictive than Coca Cola or Fanta Orange—and the ability to stay out late without worrying parents to death, my kids and their contemporaries had experienced a more constrained existence. In popular mythology we in North Down lived in an oasis of calm, but that had not stopped the bombers from finding their way, literally, to our front door.

Did it matter whether a person killed or injured had been involved directly on one side or the other of "the armed struggle", rather than a person wholly uninvolved but either singled out for sectarian attack or becoming the victim of a random or misdirected attack? Young men had died in the cause of the IRA or the UDA or the UVF, sometimes in the very act of themselves threatening the lives of others. Could a person knowingly taking these risks and willingly involved in such violence truly be regarded as a "victim" of the struggle?

I myself had always doubted the wisdom of easy rhetoric after the repeated atrocities. In particular, references to meaningless, purposeless or wholly indiscriminate violence had long given me concern. It was too easy to say "violence never achieves anything", though in some ultimate sense that may well be true, because no dream of diverse people living in amity can ever be achieved by the methods of terror. If the objective is to live in a multi-cultural society, rather than to achieve "ethnic cleansing", violence is, in that long-term sense, self-defeating. On the other hand, violence in Northern Ireland had quite clearly achieved, or helped to achieve, many intermediate political objectives: the disbandment of the Ulster Special Constabulary, the prevention of the development of its replacement Ulster Defence Regiment as a balanced force, and even in time the abolition of the Northern Ireland Parliament itself.

I remember that in the Seventies I had found myself one evening entertaining to dinner at the local Crawfordsburn Inn the London correspondent of the Soviet newspaper *Izvestia*. "May I perhaps ask you a question, Mr. Bloomfield?" "By all means." "This Irish Republican Army. Is it in your opinion a movement of national liberation, or is it on the other hand a terrorist group?" "Well, in my experience it is a terrorist group." My interlocutor paused for a moment and then observed with great seriousness: "In that case, fifteen years much too long." Somehow, as he spoke, I could hear the Russian tanks rolling down the streets of Budapest.

Yet it was not a stupid question to ask. In a situation of political/sectarian conflict, one man's terrorist is another man's freedom fighter. It is all too easy to rationalise evil means as required to promote good ends. We had republican organisations seeing themselves as breaking the yoke of British imperialism in Ireland, and regarding British soldiers or Northern Ireland policemen or women working alongside them as wholly legitimate targets in their "war". We had people who defended indiscriminate bombing in city or town centres as the best means to draw their grievances and demands to the attention of the British government, albeit with some regrettable collateral damage to uninvolved civilians. We had "loyalist" organisations persuaded that the wider Catholic community shared with republican terrorists the aspiration to Irish unity, and in their view were prepared to shelter and protect them. They therefore concluded that the murder of innocent Catholics wholly at random was the only available means to make these sympathisers think again.

What I could see very clearly, when invited to undertake the work of Victims Commissioner, was that ongoing divisions would make any project for a central memorial unacceptably divisive. If all the dead and all the incidents leading to their deaths were to be commemorated, would there not be an outcry about a lack of distinction between innocent victims and those who had sought themselves to kill and knowingly exposed themselves to risk?

What about those employed by the State and killed in pursuit of its business, particularly when serving in uniform as a soldier, policeman or prison officer? Where they themselves had killed someone, was such killing fully valid and justifiable morally and legally, taking account of the doctrine of "minimum force"? When an eighteen-year-old boy, perhaps in Northern Ireland only for a few days or weeks, took a wrong decision on the spur of the moment and under great pressure, was that a sadly inevitable consequence of the continuing terrorism and disorder, or "state violence" undertaken as a matter of policy to threaten and intimidate opponents of the state?

As I sought to reach a decision about the invitation to serve, I reflected that we had in existence in Northern Ireland extensive statutory provision and large budgetary allocations for health and social services, for the compensation of those suffering criminal injuries, and for the support of a wide-ranging infrastructure of voluntary and community organisations. Many of the main-line services were supposedly skewed towards those most in need, and indeed TSN ("Targeting social need") had a high rating amongst our overall public expenditure priorities.

Money was pouring into Northern Ireland from the European Union (under the Delors "Peace and Reconciliation" package), from the International Fund for Ireland and other sources of American generosity, and from elsewhere. We had political parties strongly represented in areas which had suffered most severely from the ongoing violence, and churches—all of them preaching the gospel of charity and generosity. Surely all the interests necessary for the support of victims were in place. So what was the problem?

Unfortunately the presence of schemes capable of delivering improvement did not of themselves assure improvement, or excuse a failure to monitor progress (or the lack of it). Those great potential vessels for change in what we call the public sector can, if one is not very careful, sail independently into the middle of a U-boat pack without the precaution of forming a convoy in which the ships move at the same speed and in the same direction.

It occurred to me then that, in almost seven years as a very senior advisor to ministers over a wide range of public services, and for much of that time as a co-ordinator of policies for those very areas in which much of the violence had occurred, the specific problem of the victims of "the Troubles" had never attracted any special notice. Like almost everyone else in the community I had plenty of examples to think about: people who had been my friends or guests or colleagues murdered or mutilated in some outrageous way. And above all else, I felt that our own most fortunate escape from physical harm in 1988 carried with it an obligation to use those fortunate years of further vigorous life to some useful effect.

So it was that when, in late October 1997, I returned to Belfast from some business in London and John Steele met me at the airport to say the Secretary of State was most keen to make an early announcement, I told him that I would undertake this sensitive task but would appreciate an early meeting with Mo Mowlam herself to discuss the modus operandi of the Commission.

When I went to see her in her office in Parliament Buildings at Stormont on 4 November 1997, a number of important issues were clarified. I would not be chairing a Commission of representative worthies hand-picked for the task and inevitably reflecting "the two traditions". On the whole this was a relief to me. I had no doubt that at some stage the Commission would encounter controversy, Northern Ireland society being what it is. But the announcement of a multi-person Commission would almost certainly lead to protests that this one had been included or that one excluded.

I might, of course, prove to be controversial in my own right. As someone earlier singled out for attack as a supposed tool of British imperialism, I could expect some nationalists to regard me as a government puppet, and some unionists to see my appointment as a cynical pacifier and as part of the ongoing "political process" about which some of them had become so dubious. I could only steer a resolute course of refusing a priori to categorise victims or to deter anyone from making representations to me. I said to the Secretary of State that, although it might seem odd to reach even a provisional conclusion before inviting or receiving any evidence, I hoped she would not see my remit as essentially to propose a national monument or memorial scheme. The casualties of any conflict were usually commemorated only when the conflict had definitively ended. Often the winning faction would err on the side of triumphalism, and the losing side on collective amnesia. Memorials to both sides are rare, although not entirely unknown. Quite certainly any rigidity of definition in the listing of names for memorial purposes could prove highly divisive. I may well have uttered for the first time on that occasion what became a central mantra in my work: "We have violence because we have division. Let us not, please, recognise the suffering in any way which could cause further division." Could I then, I asked the Secretary of State, focus above all on practical steps likely to be of benefit to those who had suffered directly or through the death or injury of those closest to them? I was happy and relieved to learn that Mo Mowlam would support me in taking this approach.

And so, in November 1997, I set about my task. I was fortunate indeed to discover that a great deal of the factual ground had already been most usefully explored. The organisation which had undertaken this difficult task was COTT (the Cost of the Troubles study), led by an academic from the University of Ulster, Marie Smyth. From the outset she was most kind and generous in sharing her findings, whether published or unpublished, with me. Academic research of this kind is absolutely invaluable, and it underlines the way in which higher education institutions can make a remarkable contribution to the economic, social and cultural development and well-being of their native place.

Without the dedication of Marie Smyth and her co-workers in COTT, the task of my Commission would inevitably have taken much longer to complete. They had analysed in particular all the deaths of the Troubles: where they had occurred; the age, gender and affiliations of those who had been killed; the organisations responsible for killings; and so on.

I will not seek to repeat here the great detail embodied in the COTT publications, or even my summary of that material which I included in my ultimate report as Victims Commissioner: *We Will Remember Them*. It is, however, necessary to highlight certain facts. First, the sheer dimensions of the trauma occurring in such a tiny jurisdiction. In area, Northern Ireland is only slightly larger than the state of Connecticut in the USA. Its total population of about 1.6 million is less than twice that of the city of Birmingham. In any analysis it has to be borne in mind that not all the deaths attributed to the Troubles occurred in Northern Ireland. There were fatalities in the Irish Republic, on the British mainland and in continental Europe as well as within Northern Ireland itself. And of course, not all those killed in Northern Ireland were permanent residents there; while soldiers of the

UDR or its successor, the RIR, were locally recruited, the Regular Army casualties occurred largely amongst soldiers recruited in Great Britain and returned there for burial. With these caveats, the period with which my Commission was concerned gave rise to some 3,585 deaths occurring in Northern Ireland. Had such deaths occurred pro rata across the whole United Kingdom, the tally of fatalities would have reached more than 120,000. Let us remember, too, that the total number of British servicemen killed in hostile action between the end of the Second World War and 1997 (including Korea, Cyprus, the Falklands and the first Gulf War) amounted to no more than 3,300 (671 of them in Northern Ireland). Finally, to give these comparisons an "Irish dimension", let us recall that the total death-toll in the Irish Free State during the Irish Civil War, whose echoes are only now fading in the Republic, amounted in all to about 4,000.

This is to speak only of the dead, not of those who mourn them or who live with their injuries. It is impossible, now, to compile a definitive record of all the non-fatal casualties, although a modest estimate shared by many experts is not less than 40,000. There is even less reliable information about the extent to which people have put their experiences behind them and returned to full physical and emotional health. The extent of post-traumatic stress is a particularly elusive factor. But there were a very large number whose sufferings were all too easy to see: the amputee, the blinded, the loved one lying for years in a coma in a near-vegetative condition, but too deeply loved and cherished to be allowed to slip away. And, of course, many more were affected by fatal or non-fatal injuries than the number of those who suffered such injuries. Around each death or injury the ripples of destruction and devastation spread out, affecting father, mother, brother, sister, daughter, son, friend. In a normal society the huge majority would not know personally in a lifetime a single person who has been murdered. This is far from being the case in Northern Ireland.

A second cardinal conclusion to emerge from the painstaking

analysis of fatalities is that long-distance conclusions about what has occurred are often simplistic to the brink of idiocy. It is too often assumed that every Protestant is a unionist tending towards "loyalism" and every Catholic a nationalist tending towards republicanism. Paramilitary organisations accounted for some 80% of the deaths, and more than half were the responsibility of republican paramilitaries. The biggest source of killing amongst Protestants had been republican organisations and almost half the deaths amongst Catholics could be attributed to loyalist paramilitaries. On the other hand, almost a fifth of the Protestants were killed by loyalist paramilitaries, and over a quarter of the Catholics by republican paramilitaries, in activities such as internal feuds or the infliction of punishment upon alleged informers. As a consequence of mistaken identity, "accidents" or the effects of random and indiscriminate violence, paramilitaries on each side had managed to murder a considerable number of people from what they would consider "their own community". A huge car bomb in a busy market town was incapable of discriminating in its choice of victims. The limp "apology" of a terrorist group for an attack on an unintended target was little consolation to the victim, if he or she survived the incident.

My task, however, was about much more than statistical analysis. The urgent need was to get close to the victims and those who sought to speak for them. My terms of reference had requested me to consult "various organisations concerned with the welfare of the bereaved and the disabled, as well as with community groups, churches and political parties". To fulfil that obligation, I placed advertisements in local newspapers, took the fullest opportunity afforded by the broadcasting media to invite views and evidence, and wrote directly to a very large number of political, ecclesiastical, statutory and voluntary organisations.

At the outset, I expected that broadly representative organisations, such as churches or political parties, would in every case take full advantage of the opportunity not only to submit written views and evidence but also to discuss directly with me the dreadful sufferings of so many of their own members. I have to say that in some cases at least the meagreness of reaction, or even failure to react at all, was a source of great surprise and disappointment to me. I could excuse a good deal of delay at the outset by the knowledge that many of these organisations had complex and bureaucratic structures ill-suited to the provision of a rapid response. What I found (and still find) extraordinary is that some of the political parties, despite repeated prompting, did not offer me a single suggestion or word of advice from start to finish, and I have often bitten my lip in later years as spokespersons for those very parties waxed vociferously and eloquently about "the victims", treating it in my view as a convenient piece of political polemic rather than a real human issue.

The response from churches was variable. Some were able to give me the great benefit of their strong international contacts, drawing for example on their knowledge of developments in South Africa. I must record that I was received with real courtesy at the Martyrs Memorial Free Presbyterian Church and had a helpful discussion of the issues with a representative of that church, although not with the Moderator himself. I was, indeed, most interested to be given a tour of the highly impressive premises.

These views, however useful, were at best second-hand. I needed to get much closer to the community of victims. Here I was given my first foretaste of what was to come in an initial interview on Radio Ulster about the Commission's work. Alongside me in the little studio I found Mrs Margaret McKinney. When I had said my piece about terms of reference and procedures and timetables—all the clinical stuff of a government review—Margaret was interviewed about the circumstances in which, as long ago as May 1978, her young son Brian had "disappeared", abducted and almost certainly murdered by a paramilitary organisation but with no knowledge of his ultimate fate or the place where his body lay. She was an utterly genuine and totally honest person. Her son, she admitted, had been to some degree a difficult and troublesome young man, but that did not diminish her love or loyalty for him, or her terrible sense of injustice that he had almost certainly been "executed" for modest misdemeanours, by nameless and unauthorised people and without any opportunity to defend himself physically or legally. A creeping sadness overtook me as I listened to Margaret's story.

Not long after this I had my first meeting with a group of those most directly affected. An organisation called WAVE had invited me to visit their offices in a converted suburban house to meet a group of those widows of the conflict for whom they sought to provide a safe haven and a place of mutual comfort. We sat in a circle, coffee or tea cups balanced on our knees, as if we were about to have a play-reading or a bible-class. One after another of these women told me their stories. The cumulative effect was initially emotional and finally numbing. For the most part they had endured years of widowhood since the early deaths by murder of their husbands. They spoke of a total absence of support or advice in the immediate aftermath. They spoke of the economic strain of keeping a household together after the death of the principal breadwinner. They spoke of the absence, until WAVE had come upon the scene, of any organisation which had seemed capable of understanding that the pain and problems did not go away over the years or decades. One woman, I remember, told me that she barely remembered the growing up of her sizeable family, so zombie-like had she been made by a continual regime of pills prescribed as the only relief of her distress. These stories were simply heart-breaking. People wept. I wept too. It was a world far removed from the comfort of the Stormont Castle office from which in earlier years I had led the civil service. I sensed that these were problems not to be solved by cool thinking and rational analysis alone.

As I left this emotional encounter still moved and shaken by the experience, I determined that the principal focus of my review, from that point on, must be to hear from the victims themselves. They had, perhaps, too often in the past—when considered at all—been used as political missiles in an endless propaganda war. So it was that I set up meetings across the length and breadth of Northern Ireland, not only in Belfast but in Derry and Enniskillen, Cookstown and Armagh. Sometimes I met particular categories of victims or their relatives; UDR widows or disabled police officers or the sufferers from a single high-profile incident like the "Teebane massacre". In most cases the meetings were open to all who wished to come.

Here and there, but not often, I encountered the accusation that I must be incapable of impartiality, as a former senior civil servant and a member of "the establishment". To such people I could only respond that they should judge the usefulness of the Commission by my ultimate report rather than by my antecedents. I listened on occasions to eloquent and obviously sincere allegations of "state violence" directed against the nationalist community, and to accusations of conspiracy and cover-up. Those who mounted such arguments were clearly less than satisfied when I explained to them that, while I could and would faithfully convey to government the sense of what they had told me and their demand for action, they could not reasonably expect me either to endorse or to reject their account of contentious circumstances which could only be unravelled, if at all, through painstaking forensic work and complex legal processes. Even as I write, the formal inquiry into a single (and certainly important, tragic and controversial) event, the so-called "Bloody Sunday" in Derry, is ploughing its way through a mountain of evidence at huge expense and with no imminent conclusion in sight.

I made a particular point of accepting the way in which our troubles had impacted upon categories of people exposed to special danger. I discussed the position of military victims with the then Chief of the General Staff, General Sir Roger Wheeler, as well as with the GOC (Northern Ireland) and Sir Denis Faulkner on behalf of the UDR. I travelled to Warrington to meet the fathers of the two young boys tragically killed there, and spoke in Manchester to some of those most directly affected by the devastating attack on its city centre.

A singular and memorable experience was my visit to Glencree Reconciliation Centre in the Wicklow Mountains south of Dublin. The Centre is in a wild and beautiful area, and gathered to meet me there were a company of those affected by the bombings in Dublin and Monaghan in 1974, carried out almost certainly by "loyalist" paramilitaries and resulting in the awful tally of thirty-three deaths. It was a long and emotional afternoon. There were some angry suggestions of collusion and cover-up but there was also a real sense of solidarity with those who had suffered in Northern Ireland, regardless of religion or politics, and an expression of appreciation that someone in authority, albeit from another jurisdiction, had come to spend time with them and listen to their story.

Of course I could not hope to meet all the victims of so prolonged and violent a conflict face-to-face. Very many, in the midst of their difficulties and distress, took the trouble to write to me. These eloquent and moving letters represent a most remarkable archive of our unhappy times, and will I hope be preserved for posterity. They are not suitable for early release, while those most affected are still living; they are too intimate, too deeply personal for that.

What I found most remarkable about them was their charity and generosity of spirit. There was, of course, no common or universal theme. Some, albeit a minority, placed a heavy emphasis on justice and retribution. I reflected upon the experience of Gordon Wilson of Enniskillen who, in the aftermath of his beloved daughter Marie's death in the Remembrance Day bombing of November 1987, had spoken in terms of Christian forgiveness and reconciliation. Many, and I amongst them, had found his broadcast words inspiring and remarkable. But that had not been a universal reaction, even from fellow-victims of the same horrific incident. There were those who expressed the sentiment: "He may forgive them, but I never will." Faced with this diversity of reaction, I came to the conclusion that it would be deeply presumptuous to criticise anyone for expressing anger as well as grief. Indeed, I reflected that we ourselves had been fortunate enough to escape from the bomb attack on our home in September 1988 with a loss of home and possessions, but without the loss of life or limb. At that time, responding to many generous letters of sympathy, I had written: "I would want all those who were in touch with us to know that we emerge with no hatred or rancour for anyone; merely with deep thankfulness that our family has been kept safe from physical harm." That was a genuine sentiment at the time. Would it, I wonder, have been the same if my wife had been dismembered, my young son blinded, or if my beloved daughter—her empty room totally lacerated by shards of glass— had been at home rather than at college in England?

Yet the greater part of this astounding correspondence expressed neither hatred nor a wish for revenge, nor put in the forefront any specific demand for compensation or reparation. Again and again an eloquent letter, often of many pages, would be in its essence a description of a loved one, an account of the circumstances in which he or she had died, and an affirmation of his value to those who continued to love and miss him. But I also became aware of what I came to think of as the loneliness of the single victim. One unforgettable letter came from the mother of a young man killed "in error" in Belfast only a day after multiple deaths had occurred at a major incident in another place. That latter episode, very understandably, was discussed with sympathy in media around the world; the names of the victims had become household words; the dependants of those victims had been singled out for private generosity on a large scale. Was her son, dying on another day and in another place, in any sense less worthy of remembrance than others?

What I learned from these letters was reinforced by the face-to-face meetings and encounters around the province. In a first period I would explain my remit, stress the need for the help and advice of those present, and ask for any comments people wished and were willing to make in front of others. Yet, I stressed, I had become well aware how emotionally draining and personally sensitive were many of the stories I wanted and needed to hear. We would, therefore, break for a cup of tea, and thereafter set time aside to meet privately any individual or family group preferring to do so. After attending one of these meetings, Martin Fletcher of *The Times* was to describe me in his newspaper as playing "the combined role of priest, doctor and agony aunt". It was not a bad description, and there was certainly no lack of agony. There was nothing in any civil service handbook to advise you that the best reaction to a weeping relative describing the worst moment of her life might well be to put an arm around her and shed a tear with her.

Each experience was unique and personal. Not surprisingly, the earliest victims of the Troubles—and the greatest number of deaths and injuries had occurred during those early years—had been the worst treated by the state and society. People had found themselves bewildered, offered little or no advice or counsel, and sometimes appalled and insulted by the modest compensation they had been offered. Police pension arrangements were much less generous than they were to become later on. In the absence of "bereavement awards" some widows had received compensation insufficient even to provide an adequate funeral, let alone help a bereaved family to resume a more or less normal life. If a woman had gone down the lane to post a letter and returned to find her shot husband dead or dying on the doorstep, she could make no claim for any subsequent mental, emotional and psychological trauma because she had not been "present at the scene". Some victims paid tribute to ministers of religion who had remained a stay and support from start to finish; others complained that they had received little help beyond the customary ceremonies of interment. Very many complained of having had to cope, when at their most vulnerable, with complex bureaucratic and legal processes they did not begin to understand. People reaching the courts to claim compensation to which they felt entitled argued that on occasions they had been treated with insensitivity and made to feel as if they were perpetrators rather than victims.

Many of these interviews were deeply poignant at a personal level. At one meeting, concentrating upon those affected by a particular outrage involving multiple deaths and injuries, I had at once noticed in the front row of the audience a wholesome, good-looking couple. Perhaps, I had thought, these were the son and daughter of one of the dead. I was quite mistaken, for when the more private interviews began and the young man limped in with his pretty wife, I realised I was meeting one of those directly involved in this horrendous explosives attack. Patiently, and without rancour, this young man told me his story. He had grown up on a farm, but had always loved the feel, the smell and the potential of wood. As a skilled carpenter in the building trade his modest but passionately held ambitions had been satisfied. His "crime" had been to join a work squad at a security force establishment. Latterly he had tried to pick up again the craft he loved and was proud of. But the explosion had left him with lungs incapable of coping with the dust of wood-working. The young man's acceptance was matched by his wife's anger. A school teacher, she had on occasions to be excused from attendance at work when her husband was at a low ebb. She felt relatively little account was taken of her special circumstances; positions of higher responsibility were withheld from her and she sensed that she was widely regarded as something of an inconvenience and even a malingerer.

At another meeting I shall never forget, an elderly but remarkably cheerful double amputee sat to talk to me from her wheelchair. "I would like to show you my arm," she said, revealing further horrible scars. Yet this was a cheerful, forward-looking woman, bereft of bitterness.

In the course of my work I saw the end result of the bullet, the car bomb or booby-trap, and the malign results of the "punishment beatings" or "punishment shootings" so freely handed out by kangaroo courts enforcing the law of a criminal mafia. In a society not much drawn to baseball as a sport of choice, baseball bats had found an unexpected market as a means of breaking bones. The young man with a limp could have been shot around the knee-caps up some dark alley, or subjected to the penetration of a Black and Decker drill. I met people who had been tortured under questioning, burned with cigarette ends, humiliated and abused in ingenious ways. In the case of our own experience in 1988, the game-plan—fortunately partly abortive—was that a series of Semtex explosive devices placed around the house would be detonated in sequence, hopefully killing or injuring such policemen as might have arrived to rescue us (as had indeed occurred in the attacks upon the army at Warrenpoint in County Down).

By the conclusion of my Commission's work, the cumulative emotional impact was beginning to tell upon me, as I often lay awake at night reflecting upon all I had seen and heard. Nevertheless, when I delivered my report, *We Will Remember Them* to the Secretary of State I concluded my covering letter with these words:

In more than forty years of public service, I have never been asked to undertake a task of such human sensitivity. The letters I have read and the stories I have heard in carrying out the work of the Commission will be burned into my memory forever. I could only describe the task you gave me as a painful privilege. painful, because I have encountered grief and human suffering on an enormous scale; a privilege, because I have encountered also such courage, such endurance and—often from those most gravely affected—such generosity of spirit.

The launch of my report at Stormont on 13 May 1998, attended by not a few of those who had shared their sufferings with me, was a uniquely moving occasion in my life. I had long felt that, although words sometimes fall short of the splendour and awfulness of human reality, the words of our poets come closest to matching the emotion of the moment. For this reason, I was deeply grateful to the distinguished local poet Michael Longley—later to be awarded the Queen's Gold Medal for Poetry—for his permission to use one of his poems as a postscript to my report, and for his willingness to read it to the company assembled that day. It was the poem I was to quote in my University Sermon at Oxford, and when Michael had finished reading it, a moving silence fell over the room. It often takes a poet to sound the depths of feeling in a unique way.

It is not my intention here to describe in detail what I recommended the government to do about the "victims issue" or how they responded to it. Unusually it was accepted immediately in principle and to some degree implemented in practice, albeit slower and with fewer resources than I would have wished. It also achieved a higher profile for the issue of the victims, both in the United Kingdom and further afield.

Not long after presentation of the report, Tony Blair visited Northern Ireland again and agreed to include in his programme a meeting at Stormont with some of those who had lost most during the years of violence. The meeting was to take place in a part of the "Long Gallery" at the west end of the Parliament Building. At the words "He's coming now", my wife and I with Adam Ingram, the "Victims Minister" designated by Mo Mowlam, moved out into the corridor to welcome and receive the Prime Minister. Looking down that long corridor I could see the youthful and vigorous Blair striding towards us at a brisk pace, with a rather substantial entourage of private secretaries, advisors, press officers and other sundry aides in tow. It reminded me, somehow, of one of those aerial shots of a new passenger liner sailing into harbour accompanied by a flotilla of small boats.

I had not met him before, but could remember being much taken years earlier by the television performance of an articulate young man, answering most questions throughout some pressing interview with formidable fluency and a pleasant smile. However, government is a very different world from opposition. We introduced those who had come to meet him, and sat in a rather stilted circle as the victims or their representatives asked their questions or made their points. I thought his performance uneven; at some times even nervous and unsure. There were, of course, angry as well as grieving people among this gathering. I had an initial impression of a person with characteristics a bit like Graeme Hick as a cricketer: on a decent wicket, and against bowling not quite of the highest class, elegant, assured and prolific, yet somehow, against really hostile bowling on a difficult wicket, Hick could seem uncomfortable, even disconcerted. It struck me that the Prime Minister did not much enjoy being criticised, or pressed with questions for which there was no ready answer. In that respect he would be much like the rest of the human race. But somehow one expected a Prime Minister to have a more impenetrable carapace. These, however, were early days in his premiership; later he would demonstrate, and need, much greater coolness under fire.

Another early visitor in the aftermath of the report was the Prince of Wales, and he too expressed a wish to meet a group of those who had suffered greatly. I thought he brought to this encounter at Hillsborough Castle extraordinary gifts of warmth, human sympathy and understanding. He listened with tremendous patience and concern, and sometimes with visible emotion, to each story of suffering he heard that day, and his parting words to me were that he would greatly like in the following year to entertain a group of the victims at Highgrove.

Interest in the report *We Will Remember Them* also led to the privilege of meeting two of the legendary figures of our time, the Czech president, Vaclav Havel, and the Dalai Lama of Tibet. It was a special pleasure to meet the revered Buddhist leader, not least because my daughter Caroline had spent some months in northern India helping to teach the children of Tibetan refugees, and had returned with a number of those white silk scarves which Tibetans drape around the necks of people they wish to welcome and honour. My respect for this saintly, pacific and delightfully jolly figure rose when he was interviewed later on Radio Derry and asked the inevitable question posed in our troubled times to all visitors of distinction. "Your Holiness, have you some advice to offer us?" "No," replied the great man, and I reflected how few of our distinguished visitors had shown such modest reticence.

***

However, my exposure to the victims issue was not yet at an end, since I found myself invited by government to carry forward two of my own recommendations: that the system of compensation for criminal injuries should be radically reviewed and that efforts should be made to persuade those with knowledge of the location of the bodies of the "disappeared" to come forward.

The question of compensation for criminal injuries was, of course, one of direct concern to many of those who had suffered most. I was very pleased, therefore, to be asked to lead a fundamental review, with the support of two most excellent colleagues in Professor Desmond Greer, an academic lawyer of distinction and an internationally recognised expert in this specific area, and Mrs Marion Gibson, a senior social work professional greatly experienced in handling the traumatic aftermath of major disasters, both within Northern Ireland and further afield.

Although our ultimate recommendations were in many cases accepted and led to some marked improvements in the law, government felt it could not go all the way with us in a central recommendation. To simplify a rather complicated issue, in Northern Ireland, unlike other parts of the United Kingdom, the general level of compensation awards was set by decisions of the courts, applying common law principles. This did not mean that all claims reached the courts—for only a minority were determined there—but rather that an approach to the courts was the last resort of an applicant for compensation dissatisfied either because his claim had been judged ineligible or had been allowed but had led to what he considered an inadequate offer. In Great Britain, on the other hand, criminal injuries compensation had been moved some years before on to a "tariff" basis, with prescribed awards for a very wide range of injuries and conditions defined in detail. Taken as a whole, the "common law" levels of awards in Northern Ireland were more generous than the tariff levels set in Great Britain.

Now in areas such as this which were not "devolved" to a local Assembly (if operating) but remained the concern of Parliament, one could not assume that particularly generous treatment for victims in Northern Ireland would never be challenged. It was also the case that, particularly where lesser injuries were concerned, we could see the real merits of a more certain, swift and less lawyer-based process. We were, however, conscious of a conviction on the part of many that, in cases where injury was so very severe as to affect the whole future life of a family, courts could be better trusted than any agency of civil government to do the right and (if justified) generous thing. And so it was that the three of us recommended a hybrid system, using a tariff basis in compensating for a wide range of less serious injuries, but keeping open access to the courts where issues and injuries of great gravity were at stake.

It was, of course, a real disappointment to us that government did not feel able to support the "hybrid" proposal. Their decision was to move to a tariff basis for all injuries, but most significantly this would not be a tariff identical with that used in Great Britain but would reflect the pre-existing (and generally more generous) level of awards in Northern Ireland.

We had faced one great difficulty in the course of our review.

Since the decision to set us up had arisen out of my report as Victims Commissioner, we were asked to focus in particular on how well or badly the system in place had served the needs of victims to date. On the other hand, we were asked by our terms of reference to recommend an improved code of law which would apply only to future cases. As our work proceeded, we identified a substantial number of cases which had led to trivial or even nil awards, quite validly under the law as it had stood at the time. People had had to live with decisions that the loss of a child which did not impact on the economic circumstances of a family did not constitute an entitlement to compensation. There were particularly hard cases before the introduction of "bereavement awards" in 1988. We were able to recommend wider availability and more generous amounts for bereavement awards in future cases; but, even though we knew very well that all governments detest the notion of retrospective awards in cases validly determined under existing law, we felt these injustices had to be brought to notice.

I myself had been favourably impressed, during a visit to Israel in May 1999, by the flexibility and relative generosity of the support available there for the civilian victims of conflict. In a society where military service is compulsory, the state felt obligated to provide generously for the long-term welfare of injured military personnel and the dependents of those killed. Extended in time to cover civilian victims also, the Israeli arrangements, allowing for regular uprating of benefits and re-assessment of categories of dependence, seemed very attractive if one had been able to start from a blank sheet of paper, but reluctantly I had to conclude that it would be unrealistic to depart so radically from British norms, when contemplating statutory changes which would have to be carried through the Westminster Parliament.

Anyone who sits on a body established to advise the government faces from time to time a moral and practical dilemma. Does one urge something which one feels to be "right" in some ideal sense, even if one is virtually certain that such proposals will prove wholly unacceptable to government and parliament? That could be regarded as quixotic to the point of folly. Does one, on the other hand, try to imagine what recommendations the government would like to have, and dress up the package in the prettiest verbal wrapping paper? That kind of abject toadyism would swiftly erode any appointee's reputation for integrity or future usefulness. What is called "the government" is very rarely, when seen from close up, a monolith. And certainly, in this review, there had been no attempt to steer us. I think on occasions you have to be prepared to stretch your terms of reference a little, if only because the true scope of a problem may not be recognised when the terms of reference are being drawn up. As a consequence you have to expect that not all your recommendations will be accepted. This should be taken in good part. Government commissions, committees and review groups are appointed to give advice to government but not to usurp its functions or those of Parliament. I am, as it happens, one of the many admirers of Chris Patten, for many years one of the most intelligent and civilised people in public life. Yet even he and his able and experienced colleagues must have been surprised that their report on the future of policing in Northern Ireland was accorded in some quarters the status of the Ten Commandments or the Book of Mormon and not to be exposed to the indignity of any modification by the elected representatives of the people.

In the course of the Criminal Injuries Review I met again quite a number of those people and organisations I had earlier consulted as Victims Commissioner; but this time from the very specific perspective of the economic disadvantages they had suffered as a consequence of violence, often over many years, with adverse effects upon quality of life including the educational and other opportunities open to children of the family. This evidence persuaded us to argue that, if a retrospective topping-up of earlier compensation awards was

[163]

ruled out, other means should be sought within a comprehensive policy to assist those "left behind" by later improvements in the compensation code. This is a matter for the new Commissioners appointed in 2008.

***

My final task in facing the effects of violence has proved the most sensitive and difficult of all. In *We Will Remember Them*, I had singled out what I called the poignant category of "the disappeared". "While this report has been commissioned by and made to government," I wrote, "I would voice a fervent appeal, on behalf of those whose loved ones have disappeared without trace, that those who can offer information about their fate and where bodies may lie should now do so. I realise that many of those in possession of such information may fear the risk of inculpating themselves, but I am sure cast-iron arrangements could be made, if necessary through trusted intermediaries, to report such information anonymously and in confidence. Many of the relatives have faced up long ago to the probability that a loved one has been killed, but it is one of the most fundamental human instincts to seek certain knowledge of the fate of a husband or wife, son or daughter, brother or sister. Common humanity cries out for this modest act of mercy."

Subsequent to writing these words, I took every opportunity open to me, whether in press or broadcast interviews or in writing articles for newspapers, to keep this problem on the front burner. It was already all too apparent to me that the bargaining about future political organisations and processes had not been accompanied by any marked growth of mutual trust and confidence between people and communities so long at odds. While still in office as a civil servant, I had come across very often—not least around the time of the Anglo-Irish Agreement of 1985—an emphasis upon the need for "confidence-building measures". Local political parties, it had long struck me, were very good at arguing their own cause and formulating their own demands, in some cases with the monotonous regularity of some oriental chant or mantra. They had so far given piteously little evidence of willingness or ability to ask themselves the question: "Why are these other people so suspicious or afraid of us? Is there anything we could do, without departing from our basic principles or ultimate objectives, to build some degree of confidence on the other side?" In particular, parties which had never deviated from democratic methods or associated with private armies looked—usually in vain—for some convincing evidence that a new dawn was truly breaking after three decades of darkness. In the case of "the disappeared", the finger of (usually well informed) suspicion pointed towards the involvement in abduction and murder of republican paramilitaries. I have already pointed out that we were not dealing with anything so simple as a "war" between Protestant loyalists and Catholic republicans. In this instance, most of the "disappeared" were themselves members of the Catholic community, assumed to have offended republican paramilitaries in some way and as a consequence brutally murdered without any element of law or due process. The "crime" rendering one liable to this summary execution could be something as simple, in our allegedly Christian country, as comforting a dying soldier in the street.

At last constant reiteration, by myself and others, produced belatedly what seemed a promising response. Speaking on Radio Ulster on 13 August 1998 I had said: "I think it is awful that there continue to be hints that the whereabouts of the disappeared are about to be disclosed and somehow nothing ever happens. I see speculation in the papers that things are moving in that direction, that there may be an announcement some of these days. I would say, if you are going to do it, get on with it." The following day, 14 August, there was a significant statement from the then current chairman of Sinn Féin, Mitchel McLaughlin. Describing the whole issue as "emotive", McLaughlin continued: "It is clearly understood that this is an important and extremely sensitive matter and one which must be resolved if a proper process of grieving and healing for the families is possible. I would urge any individual or groups possessing information on anyone who is missing to provide the families involved with that information. For our part Sinn Féin will continue to speak out in support of the families concerned ... The basic human requirement to mourn and honour those we have lost is universally acknowledged and accepted."

No doubt some of the relatives of the "disappeared" swallowed hard on receipt of this assurance that a party with such a close relationship with the killing machine would "continue" to speak out on their behalf. But since it seemed reasonable to assume that Sinn Féin was in a stronger position than most of us to "urge" the anonymous individuals or groups to come forward, I found Mr McLaughlin's positive reaction to my plea to be encouraging.

The precise number of the "disappeared" is, of course, partly a question of definition, but the generally accepted number is around sixteen. Between Mr McLaughlin's statement of August 1998 and March 1999 it became clear that PIRA would make available certain information about the resting places of a number of its victims if, but only if, Sinn Féin could be assured of immunity from prosecution for those involved. This period culminated in March with a PIRA admission that they had information in relation to nine people they had abducted and killed during the Seventies and Eighties. They claimed at that time that most of those they had killed had been giving information to the security forces, an allegation vehemently denied in most cases by the victims' families. They did, however, acknowledge "incalculable pain and distress" felt by such families over a protracted period.

I myself, as I have said, had acknowledged in my report as Victims Commissioner that people were unlikely to come forward with useful information which could inculpate themselves, and had expressed confidence that "cast-iron arrangements could be made, through trusted intermediaries, to report such information anonymously and in confidence". While the victims at issue had generally been abducted within Northern Ireland, there could be no certainty about the precise location of any further crime committed, or about the place chosen for the disposal of a body. These realities made it obvious that arrangements for a credible and comprehensive scheme of recovery would have to be in place in both Irish jurisdictions.

On 29 March 1999 the Secretary of State for Northern Ireland, Mo Mowlam, announced the government's intention of introducing legislation to ensure that any evidence which might emerge in locating the remains of the "disappeared" could not be used in subsequent legal proceedings. Such legislation would be designed to facilitate the provision of information about the whereabouts of remains to an international Commission, to be established by treaty between the British and Irish governments. This announcement was followed up by the introduction into the House of Commons on 28 April 1999 of a Northern Ireland (Location of Victims' Remains) Bill and by the introduction into Dáil Éireann of a matching piece of legislation, the Criminal Justice (Location of Victims' Remains) Bill.

These legislative steps followed hard upon an Agreement between the two governments, made on 27 April, to establish an Independent Commission for the Location of Victims' Remains. The Bills gave statutory backing to the establishment of such a Commission; provided for various forms of protection to attach to information furnished to the Commission (and any evidence which might come to light as a result) about the whereabouts of the remains of victims; and made provision in relation to the entry and search of premises where remains were likely to be found.

In the course of its passage through both Houses of Parliament the British Bill did not escape substantial criticism, largely from the Unionist and Conservative benches. It was strongly argued that it was totally wrong in principle to provide for people guilty of the most horrendous crimes of the "Troubles" effective immunity from prosecution. The response of government was two-fold: first, that it was absolutely clear that, without the kind of immunities offered under the controversial legislation, there was virtual certainty that no information helpful to the suffering relatives would ever come forward; and second, that those involved in such killings were not being afforded absolute immunity from prosecution, but a more limited immunity relating solely to the information and evidence flowing directly from the work of the Commission.

I could well understand the distaste expressed by various critics for the remedies proposed in the Bill, although they had to be seen in the context of the progressive release from prison, under the terms of the Belfast (Good Friday) Agreement of many people who had already been convicted under due process for the most horrendous murders. Moreover, the Commission would be seeking useful information about people abducted in the Seventies, and if no information adequate to bring anyone to trial had emerged over all that time, the limited immunity could be regarded as more of a gesture than an impediment to arrests and prosecutions. Above all, there was the pain and endless uncertainty experienced by the relatives like my friend (for such she had now become) Margaret McKinney.

While all of this drama was being played out on the political stage, Adam Ingram, designated "Minister for Victims" following my Commission report, took me to one side at a social event. The new Independent Commission would have two members—one from the United Kingdom and one from the Irish Republic—who would be appointed shortly by the two governments. Would I be willing to go forward as the British nominee? I could see at once that such an assignment would immerse me once again in the most sensitive and emotive issues. But as I myself had again and again made appeals for progress on this front, I felt an absolute obligation to accept.

The political and governmental processes were completed on

28 May 1999 when, by agreement between the two governments, the Independent Commission for the Location of Victims' Remains assumed its responsibilities, and the Secretary of State for Northern Ireland and the Minister for Justice, Equality and Law Reform in the Irish government jointly appointed Mr John Wilson and myself to be the members of that Commission.

I was very happy that I would find myself once again co-operating with John Wilson, a former Tanaiste (or Deputy Prime Minister) of the Irish Republic. I recalled that not long after *We Will Remember Them* had been published, and bearing in mind in particular the victims of the Dublin and Monaghan bombings I had met at Glencree in the course of my work, I had contacted an old friend in the senior ranks of the Irish civil service to say that I would be most happy to discuss my findings with the Taoiseach, if he should wish to see me. I had appreciated the fact that, in spite of predictable nit-picking from certain quarters, he and his colleagues had given my report a warm welcome and a positive response. This contact produced an invitation to meet Bertie Ahern in his office in Dublin. I had found him—as most of his visitors did—relaxed, friendly, informal and genuinely interested in what I had to tell him. My work had, perhaps, brought home to him more vividly the reality that the "victims issue" was not one for Northern Ireland alone. And so it came about that an Irish Victims Commissioner was appointed in the person of Mr John Wilson, formerly a prominent member of Irish cabinets, and served by Eamon Mulligan, who was seconded from the Department of Justice for the task. At an early stage in their work, they had invited me to share with them some of the impressions gained as Northern Ireland Victims Commissioner, and I had been very glad to do so. I was now to have the pleasure of working more closely with them. As official back-up for myself I could draw upon the services of the head of the Victims Liaison Office (VLU) set up in the Northern Ireland Office to support Adam Ingram as Victims Minister in implementing my report.

As the Independent Commission assumed its responsibilities,

we expected an early flow of information, through responsible intermediaries, from PIRA, hopefully leading to the early recovery of the nine bodies. In practice, the active phase of the recovery process developed in a wholly unexpected way, and was revealed to me in the most bizarre of circumstances. Since the visit of the Prince of Wales in 1998, I had been regularly in touch with Stephen Lamport, then Private Secretary to Prince Charles, about the Prince's wish to entertain a group of the Northern Ireland victims at Highgrove, his country house in Gloucestershire. Plans for this visit proceeded on the most sympathetic and thoughtful basis. Thanks to the great generosity of a hotelier involved with the Prince's Trust, the entire party would be accommodated gratis in London on the night of 27 May, after a memorable day which had involved a privileged visit to Windsor Castle (including parts of the Castle wholly closed to the general public), an evening visit to a West End show and a reception with the cast afterwards. My wife Elizabeth, who had made a point of accompanying me to many of my difficult and emotional meetings with groups of victims, travelled with the party from Belfast, while I was able to join them in the evening after a day spent on BBC business.

After this wonderfully generous and enjoyable start to their visit, the whole party (some of whom had seldom been out of Northern Ireland before) boarded a comfortable coach next morning for the journey to meet the Price of Wales in Gloucestershire. Amongst the company was, yet again, Margaret McKinney, mother of the "disappeared" Brian McKinney, whose story had made a powerful impression on Prince Charles the year before. As I sat in the coach chatting to Billy Stevenson, the VLU head, both about the programme for that day and about the prospects for the recovery of a substantial number of bodies, the VLU phoned Billy from Belfast with the wholly unexpected news that, following a tip-off directly to the Garda Síochana (the Irish police service), the body of one Eamon Molloy had been found left in a coffin in a graveyard at Faughart, County Louth.

Molloy, from the Ardoyne district of Belfast, had disappeared in 1975 after being accused by the IRA of being an informer. In yet another striking illustration of the perverse complexity of the situation, Eamon Molloy's brother, Anthony, at the age of eighteen, had been murdered by loyalist gunmen in Belfast. There was no rational explanation, then or subsequently, for the restoration of a body without using the privileged channel of the Commission. The limited immunity from prosecution, after all, extended only to information furnished to the Commission and any evidence resulting from it. Nevertheless, it was a relief to see some initial evidence of a genuine wish to make the recovery process effective.

But the disclosure of such information at such a time and in such a setting presented Stevenson and myself with a very real dilemma. We felt very strongly indeed that Margaret McKinney, like all the other members of our little party, deserved to have a memorably enjoyable and unclouded day in the midst of all their sorrows and concerns. On the other hand, if we said nothing, and Margaret came to hear of this news by another route, it might well damage or even rupture the confidence between us. On balance we decided that Margaret would have to be told on arrival at Highgrove but before the meting with the Prince of Wales. I am very happy to recall that, when given the news, her very characteristic response was to express the hope that the Molloy family would now enjoy some sense of closure.

We duly arrived at Highgrove House, were given a conducted tour of those delightful gardens in which the Prince of Wales takes such evident pride and pleasure, before moving into the hospitality suite where, over drinks, the Prince himself spoke with the greatest sympathy and understanding to everyone present. So warm and friendly was he that some of those who had been in a degree of dread about a very formal encounter loosened up and spoke very freely of their experiences. There were some tears, but also a lot of laughter. The party then sat down to share with the Prince a lunch which would have graced any reception for an ambassador or a visiting Head of State. In one sense these were very ordinary people, made special by the awfulness of the experience they had undergone, and treated throughout by the Prince of Wales as very special indeed. No use was ever made of this unique occasion to boost the Prince's image, so often—it seems to me—perceived through a distorting mirror.

Afterwards the party and Elizabeth returned to Gatwick for a return flight to Belfast, while I spent the next night in London, before leaving the next day for a very short visit to Canada on BBC business. Meanwhile the carefully orchestrated processes of the Commission were getting under weigh. On that same Friday, 28 May 1999, intermediaries who had been briefed on behalf of PIRA got into touch with the Commission's officer in Dublin, Eamon Mulligan. These intermediaries had received information purporting to bear on the fate of a further eight victims. In every case the information pointed to a burial in the Republic across the border, and over the weekend Mulligan was taken by the intermediaries to visit and inspect six different potential sites in Counties Louth, Monaghan, Meath and Wicklow. Not very surprisingly, the sites at issue were for the most part in remote and rough terrain, involving Mulligan, on this bizarre assize, in a task which was physically as well as emotionally demanding.

The body of Jean McConville was allegedly buried at Templetown Beach, near Carlingford in County Louth. Mrs McConville's case was a peculiarly distressing one. A mother of a large family from Divis Flats in Belfast, Mrs McConville, then still aged only thirty-seven, had disappeared in March 1972 after being abducted from her home by a twelve-strong IRA gang. Brought up as a Protestant, she had converted to Catholicism after her marriage to a Catholic. The reason for her abduction was never wholly clear. Republicans had said or implied that she had been supplying information to the security forces. On the other hand, there were those who related her disappearance to her charitable efforts to help and comfort a gravely wounded British soldier. Whatever its motivation, her abduction and disappearance had had the most appalling effect through the dispersal of her large family.

The intermediaries had been told that Brian McKinney (son of Margaret) and John McClory would be found in bog land at Colgagh in County Monaghan. McKinney, then aged twenty-three, and McClory, aged only seventeen, had left their homes at Andersonstown in Belfast, to go to work on 25 May 1978 but had never arrived there. They had both been abducted by the IRA the previous week, questioned about an armed robbery, and released. There were suggestions that IRA weapons had been "stolen" for use in robbery for personal gain. It appeared probable that the young men were kidnapped on 25 May, subjected to further interrogation and promptly "executed" or shot while trying to escape. Earlier there had been a tip-off that these bodies might be found in an area close to the Colin Glen estate in West Belfast, but a search by the RUC had turned up nothing of relevance.

Another very young man, seventeen-year-old Columba McVeigh from Donaghmore, in County Tyrone, had been abducted by the IRA, allegedly after confessing to acting as an "army agent" in attempts to infiltrate that organisation. His remains, the intermediaries had been informed, could be sought at Bragan in County Monaghan.

Brendan McGraw, twenty-four-years-old, from Belfast, had disappeared in 1978, allegedly after confessing to a role as "a British provocateur and MRF member". The advice was to seek his body in Oristown bog in County Meath.

Very similar allegations had been made against Seamus Wright and Kevin McKee of Belfast, interrogated and murdered in 1972 and to be sought at Coghalstown in County Meath.

Finally, Danny McIlhone of Belfast had disappeared in 1981, allegedly after admitting to stealing weapons.

It is worth noting that, at the time of these killings, neither jurisdiction in Ireland maintained the death penalty, even for those found guilty of heinous crimes after due process.

Some comments should be made about those who featured in this "search list". The first is that it certainly did not list all the people who had disappeared during "the Troubles" and whose precise fate remain unknown. There was no mention here of Gerry Evans, a twenty-four-year-old from Crossmaglen, who went to a dance in Castleblaney in March 1979. He was last seen hitching a lift on the Castleblaney/Crossmaglen Road just inside the Irish Republic. Amongst those who had searched for Evans in vain was Charlie Armstrong, who lived in the same estate. Two years later, in August 1981, Armstrong, then aged fifty-seven and the father of five children, went to mass and never returned home. Seamus Ruddy, aged thirty-three, from Newry, and a former member of the Irish Republican Socialist Party and the Irish National Liberation Army (INLA) had moved to Paris after the hunger-strikes, and was widely believed to have been abducted, murdered and buried somewhere in France.

All of the above could have been classed as republicans or nationalists living in republican-dominated areas. None of this could describe Captain Robert Nairac, an intelligence officer attached to the Grenadier Guards, whose brave and hazardous attempts to enter republican areas and penetrate republican organisations brought about his death at the age of twenty-nine, in May 1977. After attracting suspicion in the Three Steps Inn, in South Armagh, he had been abducted in the car park, interrogated (very probably under torture) and murdered. The Captain was posthumously awarded the George Cross.

It was clear that the sites identified to the Commission related only to people for whose death the Provisional IRA was prepared to accept responsibility, while arguing justification. Other republican organisations had not come forward, nor had any loyalist organisation admitted to a killing after abduction.

Nevertheless, on that first weekend one body, that of Eamon Molloy, had already been recovered and there seemed to be a reasonable prospect of recovering up to eight more. Since all the declared sites were in the Irish Republic, the next step for the

Commission was to brief the Gardaí, who now had to assume lead responsibility in the search for remains. Once again Eamon Mulligan had to undertake the ghoulish task of walking the ground, this time with police officers, to ensure that the information given by the intermediaries was communicated to them in all its fullness. This he now did, and with a real sense of urgency the searches got under weigh.

This was no easy task. The killings in question had occurred a long time ago, and no one could be sure in what condition remains might be recovered (although bog land in Ireland and elsewhere has shown remarkable properties in the preservation of material objects or human or animal remains). Perhaps, more significantly, the terrain itself could have changed greatly after a quarter of a century. In the case of alleged burial by the sea-shore, inroads by the sea and the impact of wind and tides upon dunes could have greatly changed the whole aspect of the location. In bog land, new bog roads could have been cut to recover the turf, and old roads abandoned and overgrown. Trees existing in the Seventies could have been felled, or clear views remembered from an earlier time obscured by new growth. We could not know by what precise means the chosen intermediaries had been given their information. A victim might have been abducted by one group, murdered by a second and interred by a third. We were completely in the dark as to whether a particular victim had died at or close to the alleged burial spot (as seemed most likely) or been conveyed as a corpse from across the border. One could safely assume that the interments themselves had been hugger-mugger activities—undertaken in wild surroundings and in thinly populated areas and brought to a conclusion as soon as possible for fear of discovery. Not many involved in such a disposal would necessarily, at the time, have given a high priority to establishing reference points for the future. The protagonists or some of them might be dead or otherwise unavailable.

Then there were the daunting physical handicaps to be

overcome. In some cases the necessary heavy equipment could not be moved onto the site without constructing very rapidly, and at not inconsiderable cost, a new roadway to the spot. In other cases, Ireland being what it is, the main impediment was the continuous flow of water into and through the site, making it essential to draw on professional skills capable of keeping a site dry enough to be excavated. Even so, heavy vehicles weighing many tonnes were in real danger of sinking into almost bottomless bog.

I took an early opportunity to visit a number of the sites. This helped me to appreciate not only the inherent difficulty presented by so much of the terrain, but also the painstaking and professional approach of the Gardaí. Understandably various relatives of disappeared persons wished to view a site where a loved one allegedly lay; some, indeed, and in particular members of the McConville family, virtually camped out on the site. The police on the spot were, I found, dealing with these deeply troubled people in the most sympathetic and understanding way. I was astonished by the scale of operations, much more closely resembling open-cast mining than the hackneyed scenes too often seen on television of some local police force digging up a modest suburban garden on suspicion of a single or multiple killings. Here huge quantities of earth were being moved, with each single bucketful meticulously inspected for any possible fragment of human remains, clothing or any other clue. In many cases, quite early in the search process, work was going on well beyond any area indicated by the original information reaching the Commission. Relatives, very understandably, would say "I sense he's here somewhere. I know he's here somewhere. Just carry on with what you are doing for a few more days or weeks, for a few more yards, metres or tones." What was depressing was the absence of positive results even where the information provided had seemed pretty clear and specific. After three weeks the searches at Ballynultagh and Oristown were suspended pending further investigation, and after consulting together John Wilson and I agreed to invite relatives to a meeting at the Ballymascanlon Hotel outside Dundalk where we could, with the assistance and support of the Gardaí, report on the work carried out so far and discuss the merits of persisting with those searches still going on.

I have earlier commented on the bizarre circumstances in which I learned of the recovery of Eamon Molloy's body. On 29 June 1999 John Wilson and I were closeted in the hotel with an understandably anxious and emotional group of relatives, and with the police officers using excellent aerial photographs to show the extent of the work involved, when one of the senior Gardaí officers was called to the telephone. He returned with the news that human remains had just been found at Colgagh in County Monaghan at a point some eighty metres away from the originally indicated search centre. In the light of the information supplied to us, it seemed virtually certain that these would prove to be the remains of Brian McKinney and John McClory. To the understandable frustration of the relatives, this could not be confirmed without painstaking and time-consuming forensic examination; but when the results became available, two families at last had remains positively identified and available for Christian burial.

It goes without saying that these discoveries re-animated the entire process. Initially the Colgagh site near Cullaville in East Monaghan, and just over the border from South Armagh, had seemed to be one of the better defined in terms of the information supplied to the Commission, relating to a distinctive and recognisable "bowl" in an area of bog land. However, the pervading ground conditions had been dreadful, and massive drainage operations had been necessary to allow the work of the Garda to proceed. By 29 June excavations had moved well beyond the central point indicated, and there was growing pessimism that the search would be successful. The subsequent discovery encouraged the belief that the Commission had not been deliberately misled, but that for various reasons the information provided had not been wholly reliable.

Encouraged by the outcome at Colgagh, the Commission asked the Gardaí to reassess plans, with the outcome of a continuation or resumption of searching at all the remaining sites for a further three weeks. By the conclusion of this period they had excavated 5,000 square metres at Templetown Beach to a depth of nine feet; a further 5,000 square metres at Bragan; 10,000 square metres to a depth of fourteen feet in Oristown bog; 25,000 square metres to a depth of seven to fourteen feet at Cogglestown; and 3,800 square metres before reaching bedrock at Ballynultagh. At the point of discovery at Colgagh excavation had taken in some 4,000 square metres to varying depths.

At the conclusion of this further fruitless period of three weeks, John Wilson and I met family members once again. We explained that, in our view, and in the professional view of the Gardaí, everything possible and reasonable had been done on the basis of the information so far available to the Commission. We felt that further searching could only prolong the agony; but we promised that we would do our best to seek further information, and if this became available and seemed to offer any reasonable prospect of success, we would not hesitate to press for resumed activity on some or all sites.

By this point in 1999, exposure to the relatives of the disappeared had underlined quite unmistakably the appalling nature of the pressures bearing upon them. The missing loved ones they hoped to recover had almost certainly been murdered without due process; in many cases the alleged "offences" against republican codes of silence and solidarity were deeply resented and disputed; the demarche by PIRA had raised real hopes of some sense of closure; any abandonment or interruption of searching could leave the awful feeling that just a little more would bring success, that next day or the day after there would be news of a discovery. For our part we as Commissioners had to be conscious of the immensity of the efforts already made, and the real risk of keeping relatives in endless suspense during excavations reaching further and further out from the original locations described to us.

Even for us in the Commission itself, who had no relatives to seek, our visits to the sites had proved a desolating experience. There was a lonely bleakness about some of these places where bodies were supposed to lie. As the great diggers clanked and bit into the soil or the bog, and as the police painstakingly inspected each bucketful of earth, one felt intensely for the relatives and their truly awful state of suspended hope. Nowhere did this atmosphere prevail so strongly as at Templetown Beach. On a normal summer's day, local people must have driven down to the car park, perhaps to picnic beside the sea. Now the whole of that car park had been torn up and excavated, with digging continued well beyond its extent and into the dunes. Here members of the McConville family kept a constant vigil. They expressed absolute conviction that the body of Jean McConville lay there somewhere and if the official searching ended they intended to carry on with their own. The love and loyalty for their mother felt by those who had been young children all those years ago was truly inspiring, and they had created at the site something approaching a mini-shrine.

All of this would have been an even more onerous task had it not been undertaken in such admirable company. I had already formed a high opinion of the men of the Garda Síochana during the dangerous years when I had been under their protection while visiting the Republic. Our briefings for the families and our visits to the designated sites had involved contact with senior officers and local Gardaí alike. Their good judgment, patience and human concern had been exemplary. Within the Commission itself, because of the focus of activity in the Republic, much of the day-to-day responsibility had been carried by Eamon Mulligan, a jewel from the Department of Justice. In my own involvement, Billy Stevenson had been as ever efficient and humane. Above all, I had developed an exemplary working relationship with my fellow Commissioner, John Wilson. A large man with a fine head of wavy grey hair, he had seemed at the first encounter the quintessential Irish countryman, certainly shrewd but possibly rather insular in his views and interests. A closer relationship showed this to be a most shallow judgment. As a former minister he had travelled widely, and had a deep and scholarly interest in language and literature, which made him, in short, the most excellent company. His earlier and wider work as the Irish Victims Commissioner had developed in him a genuine sympathy for all who had suffered. He and I were to join together on a later occasion to make a presentation to ex-senator George Mitchell to mark his tireless work for peace and reconciliation.

The cessation of work at the remaining sites was to represent a pause, not an abandonment. Towards the end of August 1999 the Commission was encouraged to believe that some additional and clarifying details would be made available through the established channels of communication, and indeed, between late August and early October of 1999, such further information was received and assessed. Following discussions with the Gardaí, the Commission decided that the process could best be moved forward by a series of specific requests for information to be passed to the informants through the intermediaries. When answers to these further queries were received, a judgment would have to be reached as to whether any or all of the sites should be reopened.

While this was going forward, the Commissioners held yet another meeting with relatives on 14 February 2000. We told them that, although further advice from the police was awaited, we felt that some resumption of searching would almost certainly be justified. We were not, however, in favour of searching without rational focus, and we had to bear in mind the impact of ground and weather conditions upon any return to the sites. We made it very clear that, while the Commission would not be considering any resumption of searching without some reasonable prospect of success, it could not be taken for granted that even in that event there would be a successful outcome.

On 28 April 2000, then, the Commission announced publicly that, after consultation with the Gardaí, searches for the remains of the victims at five named sites would be resumed on Tuesday, 2 May. However, these further searches would be information-based rather than speculative; limited in scope and in no event would be continued for more than three weeks. In the event, these further searches were abandoned on 20 May, the Commission and the Gardaí being satisfied at that point that all reasonable steps to follow up the information made available from start to finish had been taken.

However, early in 2001 the family of Charlie Armstrong, who had disappeared from Crossmaglen in 1982, received information purporting to indicate the location of his remains. In June of that year, the Gardaí, using probes and dogs, investigated a site in south east Monaghan but without results. A further limited search undertaken by the Gardaí in May 2002 was, once again, unsuccessful, as were subsequent searches mounted by the family in 2003.

Again in 2003, the Gardaí received further information in relation to the remains of Jean McConville and Columba McVeigh. However, while this information was still being assessed, Mrs McConville's remains, missing since 1972, were discovered accidentally by a family walking not on Templetown Beach, upon which so much fruitless effort had been concentrated, but on the neighbouring Shelling Hill Beach. This was in spite of the fact that information provided through intermediaries had consistently referred to Templetown, and this information had been re-affirmed when the Commission sought clarification.

John Wilson and I with Elizabeth attended the funeral mass for Mrs McConville and her subsequent interment. While recovery of her remains at long last had brought some relief, the huge damage caused to the extended family by the original killing and the subsequent saga of hopes raised and dashed was all too apparent. The claim of justification based on her alleged role as "informer" was not withdrawn; and indeed when the Police Ombudsman made it clear in 2006 that she could find no trace of such activity, the PIRA reaction was to repeat its slur.

In September 2003 the Gardaí undertook a search for the remains of Columba McVeigh, but once again without success. The disappointment and frustration of the Armstrong and McVeigh families can well be imagined. I made a point of visiting members of the Armstrong family and the mother of Columba McVeigh, and experienced at first hand the poignancy of hopes raised only to be dashed in a negative outcome.

The Commission could not be certain of further discoveries and debated whether our continuing activity might risk prompting expectations of better outcomes in the future. On balance, though, it seemed best at least to demonstrate to families that everything humanly possible was being done to recover their loved ones. This led to the engagement by the Commission in 2005 of an expert in investigative sciences, who was commissioned to review all the information received and activity undertaken to date, and to follow up any new leads, with a view to recommending what, if any, further steps should be taken. It was hoped that this might also provide a new setting in which further and better information might be made available by those with knowledge of the disposal of the bodies.

Early in 2006 John Wilson retired, to be replaced as co-Commissioner by Frank Murray, a former Secretary to the government in Dublin. We were able to consider the fruits of the expert's work, and to make recommendations to the two governments about further action by themselves and the Commission. On 3 August 2006 Frank Murray and I were able to meet a gathering of relatives in the offices of WAVE to give them advance notice of imminent announcements by the British and Irish governments.

The key elements were these. The investigative expert would

be retained by the Commission over the longer term, and colleagues from the Gardaí and the Police Service of Northern Ireland would join him in a new project team within the Commission which would take forward a new programme of work. A PO Box and confidential telephone line would be set up to receive relevant information. There would be non-invasive surveys at all suspected gravesites, including examinations of all relevant contemporary mapping, forestry records and aerial photography of sites for comparison with current imagery and mapping by imagery analysts. If need be, other experts and/or resources could be drawn into the project. Efforts would be made to collect DNA, and any surviving medical and dental records would be secured. The Commission would designate a family liaison officer, and establish a media contact point.

In our meeting with the relatives, we made it clear that in future no physical excavation of a gravesite would be undertaken unless and until the Commission had satisfied itself that there existed a good prospect of a successful recovery of remains. We emphasized, too, that past experience proved that a successful outcome could never be assured. In spite of these cautionary words, those present welcomed the decisions of the Commission and the two governments as representing a step-change from being a privileged conduit for information to adopting a more pro-active role.

The question may be asked whether the return from operations conducted since 1999 has justified the costs involved in them. By this I do not mean financial costs alone, although these must have been very substantial. The direct costs of the Commission itself, prior to its 2006 enhancement of role, supported as it was by civil servants with other duties, have been relatively modest, but the full true cost of Gardaí time and effort and of the supporting work by other authorities in the Republic must have been very substantial. By the conclusion of the first phase of work on 20 May 2000, some 85,300 square metres had been excavated, and the product painstakingly examined. In two national parliaments extraordinary legislation had been enacted, conferring upon the perpetrators of horrible crimes a limited degree of immunity. Unhappily, what is to a degree repugnant may also sometimes be necessary. The eventual outcome of all these legislative, governmental and police efforts had been at best disappointing, in that only four of the nine bodies for which PIRA accepted responsibility had been recovered, and only two of these by excavations resulting from the Commission's work.

Disappointing certainly, but disproportionate to the efforts involved? Here one moves from the realm of government into that of philosophy. What is the value to be placed, not just on the human life while it is lived but on a human body from which life has departed? At the conclusion of many great conflicts, nation states have gone to immense trouble and expense to ensure for combatants, wherever possible, a decent burial, or even to "bring the boys home". As I have pointed out, the families involved in these painful events came overwhelmingly from that Catholic tradition which attaches such importance to a Christian burial and the ceremonies and rituals associated with it. Of course all concerned would have wished to offer solace and closure to all the families of the "disappeared", but one should not undervalue the restoration of certainty to four families at least.

Why was the exercise not more successful at the outset? Some, at least, would believe that the Commission and the two governments were simply the victims of a cynical propaganda exercise, and possibly of some deliberate misinformation. There had been persistent rumours that some of those being sought in the Republic had in fact been buried in Northern Ireland. For myself, while believing the PIRA, on its record, to be more than capable of both propaganda and cynicism, I could see no rationale for the provision of deliberate misinformation to the Commission. Sinn Féin, seeking to present itself as a wholly democratic political party, were happy to wear the cloak of "helpfulness" in the search for bodies, not least to avert attention from the horrid reality that their paramilitary associates had murdered these people in the first place and showed scant regret for this means of enforcing their nasty code. For some time the entire issue, kept under continuous public notice by the efforts of myself and others, had been a patent embarrassment to Sinn Féin. Rather was I persuaded that the recollection of events, probably undertaken in haste and at dead of night, had after so many years been hazy and incomplete. Priority for the "volunteers" on the day of burial would have been to dispose of the body, not to mark or record where it might be recovered one day.

Over time my colleague John Wilson and I had become increasingly conscious that the Commission's role was little more than a privileged conduit for information, involving a risk of creating expectations we could not fulfil. Intermediaries, briefed by representatives of those responsible for, or claiming knowledge of, the killings had come forward with information. Since all the suggested locations had been in the Republic, such information had been passed on to the Gardaí who had then undertaken searches for remains with the limited and disappointing results already described.

This is why we had recommended in our 2004 report to the two governments that the operation of the Commission should be reviewed and, if necessary, redirected. In November of that year the Northern Ireland Affairs Committee of the House of Commons announced an inquiry into "ways of dealing with Northern Ireland's past". Their report, published in April 2005, dealt amongst other issues with the question of the "disappeared". In paragraph 50 they stated: "That a significant number of the 'disappeared' remain unaccounted for, and their bodies undiscovered; that the families of the 'disappeared' feel obliged to take the opportunity afforded by this inquiry to bring their concerns and frustrations to us, in some cases over three decades since the disappearances took place; that the governments have, to date, failed in their efforts to enable these families to achieve closure for their hurt and as a result the families feel, in their own memorable words that 'We might as well disappear when it comes to it because we have to keep coming forward and saying we are still here' is very disappointing. We look to the governments for a renewed effort, and to those who have relevant information to come forward without delay ... The governments concerned need to give this issue a much higher priority."

In June 2005, as I have explained, the two governments responded positively to our request for a review with a proposal that the Commission should be funded to engage an eminent consultant in investigative sciences, Mr Geoff Knupfer, as its agent to conduct "a peer review of the searches for the location of the victims' remains that have taken place to date and evaluate if more can be done to locate these remains". John Wilson and I met the victims' families to inform them of this significant development, promised to keep them regularly in touch with progress, but coupled our hope for a degree of success with a reminder that this could not be assured.

When John Wilson and I were first appointed in 1999 I thought it likely that our work would be completed within months. While John, as his health began to fail, was obliged to resign, to be replaced by Frank Murray, I continue to serve, and have thus been involved in one aspect or other of the "victims' issue" continuously since 1997. At the funeral mass for John Wilson in Dublin, in 2007, I was movingly reminded of his versatility as scholar, teacher, sportsman and politician; truly a "renaissance man".

By August 2007, then, the remains of four victims had been recovered, either by accident, or on the basis of information available through the Commission or otherwise. The bodies of Danny McIlhone, Columba McVeigh, Charles Armstrong, Seamus Wright, Kevin McKee, Brendan Megraw, Gerard Evans and the British soldier Robert Nairac remained undiscovered, but were known or suspected to lie somewhere in Ireland. In addition the French authorities had been approached to facilitate a search for the remains of Seamus Ruddy, believed to lie in that country.

As I write, renewed efforts to locate some or all of these bodies are under weigh. With Geoff Knupfer as head of a multi-disciplinary investigative team, the most up-to-date techniques are available. The Commission cannot guarantee success; this is not within our gift. But it is our hope that, at the very least, relatives of those who "disappeared" will be satisfied that no effort has been spared to recover the bodies of their loved ones. I had them much in mind when I entitled my 1998 report *We Will Remember Them*.

I have, then, been involved in some aspect of the issue of victims and survivors for more than ten years. I have come to realise that other communities have shared the unhappy experience of exposure to terror. Indeed, in the world today no community on the globe can entirely avoid this shadow. I was intrigued to find that an organisation in Guernika had translated my 1998 report into Castillian and Basque.

In June 2007 I was surprised to receive an e-mail from Warsaw. It came to me from the Warsaw-based Office for Democratic Institutions and Human Rights (ODIHR), an arm of the Organisation for Security and Cooperation in Europe (OSCE), a product of the "Helsinki Accords". The message conveyed an invitation to act as moderator at a session of an impending "High-level meeting on victims of terrorism" to be convened in Vienna in September.

My acceptance afforded me an extraordinary and privileged experience. We met at the Conference Centre in the grand setting of the Hofburg, the huge palace complex from which the Austro-Hungarian emperors once ruled their polyglot dominions. From the moderator's seat one faced delegates from around seventy nation states, including not only virtually every European country from Andorra to Liechtenstein, but successor states of the Soviet Union like Turkmenistan or Kazakhstan, and nations further afield such as Israel and Afghanistan. In addition the meeting was attended by representatives of numerous NGOs around the world, often representing the specific interests of those affected by a particular outrage—be it 9/11, the Bali bombings or the Beslan siege. It was a moving experience not merely to listen to, but to meet, people who had suffered so much.

In the opening session, which I chaired, we addressed questions very familiar to me from work in our own jurisdiction. How can solidarity with victims of terrorism act as a factor in the prevention of further terrorism? What are the distinguishing features of victims of terrorism? Is it important to differentiate between victims of terrorism and victims of violent crime more generally? Are there risks in creating a hierarchy of victims? Could the occupation of a casualty of a terrorist act affect his or her status as a victim?

Later sessions would consider how to ensure appropriate assistance to victims of terrorist acts; how the interests of the victims can be properly represented in legal proceedings; and how the players in civil society can best promote solidarity with the victims of terrorism.

It was evident that at present the degree of support varies greatly from country to country, and that there is much to learn from best practice. What was all too clear was that any community, anywhere, can find itself coping with the after-effects of this modern scourge of indiscriminate terrorism. As one sat at the top table, confronting that huge range of national delegations, served by a battery of translators, it was to recognise the importance and timeliness of this important initiative and the broad international response to it. No one listening to the powerful and affecting stories brought to the meeting by so many could fail to appreciate the urgent need for a humane and worldwide response. In our support of those who have suffered so much we demonstrate our abhorrence of the callous methods and spurious justifications of terror. In my native Northern Ireland I have met many of the disabled, the widows, the relatives with no known grave to visit. I have stood amongst the grieving survivors in Claudy as, years after the event but with their grief unabated, they unveiled at last a memorial to their dead. As I spoke at the Hofburg to a Canadian widow of 9/11, and as I heard through the voice of a translator a personal account of the carnage at Beslan, I reflected once again on the truth of the adage, "No man is an island."

7

And Was This All?

I HAVE TRIED IN WHAT I have written to describe my involvement, almost all of it in the public sector, in a number of activities since 1991. But these things have not represented the whole of my life over a period of fifteen years. A major element in my life from 1991 to 1999 was service as the BBC's National Governor for Northern Ireland, but there is so much I want to say about the past, present and future of the Corporation that it will be the subject of a separate work. I was also employed at different times as a consultant in fields as diverse as printing and publication, property management and energy development.

Alongside this, I would have been crazy not to enjoy myself. As I have mentioned, I have written a couple of books and many articles, spoken to diverse audiences on a huge variety of topics, given away prizes at a long list of schools; all of these activities have been a pleasure rather than a chore. Throughout my longish life I have loved words and the use of words. My library has grown and grown, to my huge pleasure and edification. I have travelled widely: to the United States, Canada and Bermuda; to Spain, Portugal, the Czech Republic, Belgium, France, Hungary, Italy, Germany, Estonia, Russia, Finland and Denmark; to the Philippines and Bangladesh; and to Israel.

I have been privileged to attend a Rugby World Cup final at Twickenham, and Elizabeth has been with me to see Ulster win the European Cup in Dublin, to watch great contests at Wimbledon, including two women's finals, to be in the audience at the Last Night of the Proms, at opera or the ballet at Covent Garden, at the finals of the Young Musician of the Year and Cardiff Singer of the World, and at the BAFTA awards.

It was sad to say farewell to my father on my own sixty-second birthday when he died in his ninety-third year, but an enduring delight to see our dear daughter Caroline happily married in May 2005, with our son Timothy resplendent as an usher and busy with his camera.

But above all, my wife Elizabeth and I have experienced all these things together. It only seems yesterday since I waited for her at the altar of the Brick Church on Park Avenue in Manhattan in September 1960. For many years she had loyally supported me on occasions of official duty, not all of them a bundle of fun. She had bounced back with tremendous courage from the bombing of our home in Crawfordsburn in 1988.

In that "new life" of ours I have tried to describe here, she has made her own independent mark in a myriad of activities. A particular favourite of hers was service as one of the Trustees of the Ian Gow Memorial Fund. After this brave politician's assassination by the IRA because of his outspoken views on the Northern Ireland situation, his friends and admirers had generously raised a very large sum of money as a memorial and tribute to him. It was the wish in particular of his widow, Dame Jane, that these funds should be distributed to help young people in Northern Ireland. It was truly remarkable that, rather than turning their backs upon the occasion of Ian Gow's death, she and others wished to make a contribution to the building of a better future. Elizabeth was then invited to serve as an initial Trustee alongside people of distinction, such as Geoffrey Howe, a former Deputy Prime Minister, and Sir Peter Hordern MP. She made it her particular concern to seek out good causes and deserving recipients in Northern Ireland. Particular priorities were the support of integrated schools, especially the building up of libraries for the children, and the encouragement of musical talent. The latter was close to the heart of Dame Jane Gow herself, being an amateur pianist of some distinction.

Elizabeth, as a consequence, had the great satisfaction of seeing for herself the benefit of Fund support. She would be invited to open new libraries, or regularly attend events at places such as Hazelwood Integrated School.

Since 1991 I have found that I have quite a gift for ideleness; Elizabeth does not share it. She has revealed a singular ability to raise funds for good causes. Celebrities of all kinds have found it impossible to resist her pleas to offer their services gratis, whether to speak or to perform. At her invitation, the likes of Lord Eames, Sir Ronnie Flanagan, the pianist Barry Douglas, the flute player Sir James Galway, the broadcasters Sue McGregor and Eamonn Holmes, and the polymath Baroness Neuberger, have made themselves available to assist at fund-raising events and activities. Invitees to such occasions, in venues like Hillsborough Castle, have found it equally difficult to say no. Elizabeth would then organise with meticulous care every little detail of the event to ensure its perfection.

A particular beneficiary of these skills has been The Salvation Army. After several years as Chairman of its Northern Ireland Advisory Board, Elizabeth took the initiative of founding an organization called "Friends of The Salvation Army" and of persuading many of the most prominent people in the community to associate themselves in this way with the Army's invaluable social work for the most disadvantaged in society. Not many new organisations could boast of two Nobel Prize winners amongst its membership.

In October 2007, at a dinner held on the Jordanstown campus of the University of Ulster, Elizabeth raised £17,000 from a memorable event at which Lord Alderdice spoke to great effect. As ever it had been organised with meticulous attention to detail. So it is that her Certificate of Recognition by the Territorial Commander of the Salvation Army hangs alongside her Gold Award from Combat Cancer, another good cause which has benefited from her efforts. Her many other activities have included the Visiting Committee of the Young Offenders Centre, the boards of the Sports Council and the Spirit of Enniskillen Bursaries, and work on behalf of Bryson House and Help the Aged.

So, since 1991, Elizabeth has truly come into her own. I am enormously proud of her, constantly amazed by her unflagging energy and enthusiasm, and glad that in our "new life" she has been able to make her own distinctive and valuable contribution to our society. Alongside all she has done in her own right, I recognise that, without her, I might well have opted for an easier but less fulfilling life. Whenever I have been presented with a potential challenge, she has been the one to say: "Go for it!"

Appendix

WORDS HAVE BEEN THE RAW MATERIAL of much of my life. From my earliest days as a civil servant I was involved in writing the varied papers which are the daily fare of government; minutes of meetings, "submissions" on policy issues to ministers or senior officials, draft speeches for parliamentary or other occasions, replies to parliamentary questions, White or Green papers setting out policies or policy options. Like other skills, one learns by one's mistakes. In the Fifties, most senior officials would take up their pens to amend one's draft before actually reading it. One delightful assistant secretary of the old school would seldom miss the opportunity to give a brief lecture on punctuation. Then, in 1956, I became a private secretary and had the opportunity to write speeches for my ministerial bosses for public occasions. This privilege, however, was not without its pitfalls. The Minister of Finance, Brian Maginess, was invited to speak at a conference for university librarians in Belfast and knowing that the company at lunch would include librarians from Glasgow, Edinburgh, St Andrew's and other Scottish institutions, I inserted what I hoped would be a graceful passage as follows: "It's wonderful to reflect on the unifying power of literature. Why, even in the Soviet

Union they enjoy the poetry of Rabbie Burns." Maginess read this passage as drafted, paused a moment, and then added: "And surely that shows they're barbarians if nothing else does."

When Terence O'Neill became Prime Minister one of my duties was to write the "Queen's Speech" in which the government of the day reveals its legislative programme for the session after the State Opening of Parliament. At Westminster the government writes it and the Queen delivers it, whereas, at Stormont, the Governor read out the text prepared by the Northern Ireland government. In essence it was a pretty boring list of proposals. I recall that when O'Neill had served five years as Prime Minister, we his aides entertained him to dinner at Balloo. For the occasion I prepared a spoof Queen's Speech which included the following: "My government will bring forward proposals for the better marketing of eggs. These will be laid before you in due course."

In 1972 direct rule from Westminster was introduced, and would persist, save for the brief "power-sharing" period in 1974, until my retirement from the civil service in 1991. By 1974 I had reached the rank of permanent secretary, and over the years which followed found myself having to speak on a great many public occasions. In the past, senior civil servants could remain fairly anonymous figures. But the reality of direct rule was that one's departmental minister usually had to supervise more than one Northern Ireland department, be present in London for parliamentary debates or cabinet committees, and keep in touch with a constituency in Great Britain. For these reasons a minister might have to refuse an invitation or—having accepted it—pull out at short notice. Yet the society of this or the institution of that would still wish to have a government presence, and so the permanent secretary would be pressed into service. Like so many other tasks, public speaking becomes easier with practice, and I came to find it more of a pleasure than a chore.

Since 1991, and partly because of my continuing involvement in the matters discussed in this book, I have continued to write or speak on a great many subjects and occasions. I have appeared on television and radio, both local and national, written many articles for newspapers and magazines, and produced government reports on a range of issues, contributed to books edited by others and published two of my own, *Stormont in Crisis* in 1994 and *A Tragedy of Errors* in 2007. I have particularly enjoyed the opportunity to speak at the prize-days of numerous schools. While I often speak from short notes or "off the cuff", I have retained the full texts of some two hundred speeches from this period.

This activity has taken me to many fascinating venues; I have been privileged to speak in Oxford and Cambridge colleges, at St Patrick's Hall in Dublin Castle, at the Mansion House and Painted Chamber of Greenwich palace in London. I have also taken part in conferences in Paris and Vienna, The Hague and Dhaka.

Of these many speeches, four in particular encapsulate themes to which I have returned again and again—the threat of terrorism and the problems of victims of violence, the search for peace and stable government in Northern Ireland, and the developing relationships between Northern Ireland and the Republic.

On 12 May 1994 I launched my book *Stormont in Crisis* at the Linen Hall Library in Belfast, with Professor Paul Arthur of the University of Ulster as a guest speaker. On that occasion I said:

As the title implies, much of the book is concerned with my years at Stormont. We were still in the Fifties when I became a front-row spectator of events there, and I remained in my seat throughout the Sixties, Seventies, and Eighties and into the early Nineties. When asked what he did during the French Revolution, the Abbe Sieyes replied, "I survived." And I have written this book primarily because I believe it is the obligation of a survivor to leave behind some account of the most turbulent period in our local history. Historical study claimed me at Oxford, and I have not since wholly abandoned it. But I have not set out to be a Clive Ponting or a Peter Wright. What I have tried to do is to humanise those facts, to explain what it was like to be there. I have said more than once that the historian of the future will have an overload of documentation available to him. Yet documents are only the frail ghost of what actually occurred—and I should know, since I wrote a good many of them! I want you to understand that I never kept a diary because it did not seem fitting to be jotting down every unconsidered word uttered in confidence. I have relied very largely on memory. Inevitably I have been critical of some, because without that the book would not be honest. Nevertheless I have hated very few people. I have never been a good hater; somehow I never quite got the knack of it. By and large I have been conscious that even some of those who do the worst of things do them with the best intentions.

In some respects it is a sad story. When I was in harness people used to say to me, "You always have a smile on your face. Clearly none of this is any trouble to you." Acting, all acting. I do not believe that the leader of any organisation helps those he leads by looking miserable. In truth I was often sick at heart, full of grief for my province and occasionally close to despair.

It is an unhappy fact that when I retired in 1991 Northern Ireland was in some important respects a less happy place that it had been in 1952. People then did not have to go about their daily business in fear of their lives. Yet it would be quite wrong to imply that nothing had changed for the better. Housing had improved beyond measure; Belfast had greatly modernized and transformed; above all the old ugly rubbish of limited voting systems and inbuilt bias had been swept away.

I offer in my book no remedy for our present discontents but I do hope people will read between the lines and seek to learn something from our mistakes over those four decades. I find it stupefying that even now some of the principal figures sing the song of Edith Piaf, "I Regret Nothing". My own perception is of an endless series of missed opportunities to stabilise a deteriorating situation.

The book is also intended to be a celebration as well as a modest offering to history. It celebrates those people and those institutions which have meant most to me. First and foremost it recognizes the immense contribution made to my whole life and career by my wife Elizabeth, who has experienced all the "ups" as well as the "downs". What she has done for me merits a book to itself.

I hope too I have been able to convey something of the affection I feel for my old school, Belfast Inst, and of the debt I owe to it. There was, in the Forties, no better location in this city to be placed in contact with liberal and humane values.

Politics apart, I have tried also to show something of what it is to be a public servant. I was immensely proud of our Northern Ireland Civil Service. In my view it represented, through these trying times, a large element of the cement holding this community together. I am very pleased to see here today some of those colleagues to whom I owed so much. Public administration is after all a team game.

In 2001 I was invited by my alma mater, the University of Oxford, to deliver the University Sermon in the ancient and historic church of St Mary the Virgin. The invitation reached me from the "Summoner of Preachers", the Rev Professor Ernest Nicholson, then Provost of Oriel College, a Pro Vice Chancellor and a son of Portadown. At Oriel Elizabeth and I were entertained to a dinner attended by, amongst others, Robin Butler, Master of University College and a former Cabinet Secretary and Head of the Home Civil Service. The following day, 21 October, in full academic dress, I was led in procession into the great church. It was not long after the horrors of 9/11. I had been on holiday in the lovely Spanish university city of Salamanca when that atrocity occurred, and witnessed the horrific collapse of the twin towers on television in my hotel room. As Elizabeth and I had been married in New York, lived there for three years, returned often and loved that vibrant city, the ghastly events affected me deeply. With this in mind, and with my concern for victims of terrorism in Northern Ireland, it was not difficult to identify a theme for my sermon that day. I said:

My text this morning is taken from the third verse of the seventh chapter of the Gospel according to St Matthew: "And why beholdest thou the mote that is in thy brother's eye, but considerest not the beam that is in thine own eye."

In his autobiographical poem, "Summoned By Bells", John

Betjeman reminds us that Oxford has always been a city of churches as well as colleges. I remember very clearly my last attendance as a worshipper in this great University Church of St Mary the Virgin. With many others, led by the Vice Chancellor of the day, we had gathered here to remember with pride and sorrow the service to the nation of the late King George VI.

It would be perverse not to reflect on an occasion such as this upon the horrors unveiled to us on 11 September 2001. Myself and my wife lived for a time in the United States, and like so many others cherish a deep affection for that country and its people. On the day of the attacks I happened to be in another great city of churches and colleges, Salamanca in Spain. So it was there, through the medium of television, that I witnessed those fearsome episodes and the reaction of America and the world to them.

Many of you may subsequently have watched, as I did, the moving memorial service held in Washington's great National Cathedral. I recalled vividly that I had heard in that Cathedral on an earlier occasion a fine sermon preached by the Dean of Oklahoma City about the terrorist outrage there and the response to it.

The sickness of terrorism is rampant today in many places: is there, we ask, an antidote to it? Here I can only speak from my own experience. Ireland, where I have lived and worked from most of my life, often describes itself as a "Land of Saints and Scholars". Certainly it is a place in which Christianity has planted very deep roots. My own local town of Bangor was the seat of an ancient and celebrated abbey founded by St Comgall as long ago as 558AD, and today the Book of Bangor is a particular treasure of a continental library. Indeed, missionaries from Ireland, and not least from Bangor, were amongst the first to bring the Gospel to extensive areas of central Europe. Today, even though attendance has fallen away from its peak, the Irish, North and South, remain some of the most loyal church-going people in the Western world. Thus they have the opportunity to hear regularly those messages of peace and love which shine forth from the pages of Holy Scripture. But do they listen?

In 1997 I was asked by the then Secretary of State for Northern Ireland, Dr Marjorie Mowlan, to lead a Commission to look at possible ways of recognising the pain and suffering felt by victims of violence arising from the Troubles of the previous 30 years. When I completed that task, I used these words to describe the profound impression it had made upon me:

"In more than 45 years of public service, I have never been asked to undertake a task of such human sensitivity. The letters I have read and the stories I have heard in carrying out the work of the Commission will be burned into my memory forever. I could only describe the task you gave me as a painful privilege: painful, because I have encountered grief and human suffering on an enormous scale; a privilege, because I have also encountered such courage, such endurance and—often from those most gravely affected—such generosity of spirit."

Now all the dead and injured during more than 30 years of conflict are fewer in numbers than the casualties of a single day in New York. But ours is a small and tightly knit community, so that the death of thousands and the wounding of tens of thousands touches, as some point, almost everyone in that community. I would hope that most of us in this church today could say happily that they have never known someone who has been murdered. In Northern Ireland it is a rare citizen who can make such a claim.

I reflect that those who work in the upper reaches of a government machine can be, at times, rather remote from those they seek to govern. Certainly nothing in my previous experience had prepared me for the raw emotion of many of my encounters with victims or their relatives. I became aware of the special loneliness and vulnerability of those who mourned a loved one killed in some isolated incident of terrorist violence. The scale of an Enniskillen or an Omagh, let alone that of an Oklahoma City or a World Trade Centre, necessarily and understandably attracts the attention and the sympathy of the world. Special efforts will be made, special funds raised, special prayers said. The greatest in the land will gather to mark those deaths with a solemn dignity.

But one of the most poignant of the hundreds of letters I received came from the mother of a young student murdered—as his killers described—"by mistake" in Belfast on the day after the Remembrance Day outrage in Enniskillen. These other victims, she wrote, seem to be continually in the thoughts of the wider community. Was her son, then, to be forgotten?

I had fully expected that the greater number of the letters I would receive would press me to recommend this or that, to offer practical support of one sort or another. Some, of course, did precisely this. Yet those which spoke either of compensation or revenge were very much in the minority. Most of the letters could best be described as an affirmation of the value of an individual human life. A widow writing many years after the violent death of her husband wrote, "Here was the man I knew and the man I loved. Here was the manner of his living and of his dying. Please, please do not let him be forgotten."

My involvement in the fate of the victims was not to end with the submission of my report as Victims Commissioner. Amongst the other issues, I had highlighted the peculiarly poignant question of the so-called "disappeared"—people abducted and almost certainly murdered, but whose fate had never been known for certain and whose bodies remain "lost". Most of the "disappeared" came from the Catholic tradition, where great significance is attached to the Christian burial of a loved one. In New York, alas, many of that same tradition may never enjoy that sense of closure.

These arguments persuaded the British and Irish governments to pass through their respective parliaments exceptional legislation enabling intermediaries to pass on to members of an independent Commission information which could not be used in the prosecution of a perpetrator, and for these purposes I was appointed a co-Commissioner alongside John Wilson, a former Deputy Prime Minister of the Republic of Ireland. Information then reached us about six sites at which, allegedly, nine bodies in all had been buried. But despite the tremendous efforts of the Irish police and other authorities, only three families recovered the remains of a loved one thus leaving others in hideous uncertainty.

It is not easy to convey to you, in the calm and dignified surroundings of this great church, what it was like to visit these alleged burial sites. In a remote and waterlogged bog, or on a beach before a chilly sea, the searchers meticulously picked over tons and tons of excavated earth, sometimes in the presence of relatives who could not bear to be absent from the scene. A few photographs, a few flowers, a few rosaries might mark the spot. Really and truly one felt one was close to "the heart of darkness", and these moments swam back into my mind as I watched the desperate searches going forward amidst the ruins of lower Manhattan. The characteristics of grief have a terrible university.

Now the question has to be asked: how can it be possible for a community so overwhelmingly, so demonstrably Christian in profession, to generate such a volume of violence and grief? How, indeed, can we expect reconciliation between the Christian world and Muslim fundamentalism, or between Arab and Jew in the Middle East, if we who turn to the same Scriptures and look to the same divinity cannot resolve our squalid domestic quarrels?

The church built by man seems at times very far removed from the church ordained by God. Fission and factionalism, persecution, intolerance and sectarianism have far too long marked the conduct of the purportedly Christian world. Where I live, a scrutiny of the Saturday evening columns of the *Belfast Telegraph* offers to the prospective worshipper a positive a la carte menu of worship. It would be an impertinence to criticise any person for responding to the promptings of his or her own conscience, but it does seem unfortunate that quite so many believers seem to want above all other considerations to proclaim their superiority to and separateness from all other Christians. How many in Northern Ireland—indeed, I wonder, how many anywhere else—reach a personal judgement about the mode of religious practice after a rational examination of alternatives? For the most part, certainly in a community like ours, geography and family ties predetermine religious loyalty.

You will all have seen, I expect, the shameful pictures of children making their way to school in Belfast through a barrage of vociferous protest. I reflect on the Gospel according to St Matthew, Chapter 18, verse 6: "But whoso shall offend one of these little ones which believe in me, it were better for him that a millstone were hanged about his neck, and that he were drowned in the depth of the sea."

Of course these clashes, these conflicts, these confrontations are not really based upon fine theological distinctions. When sectarian mobs clash in Belfast it is not to hear cries of "consubstantiation" from one side or "transubstantiation" from the other. It is the evil mixture of religion with politics, and consequent struggle for power, which leads to such a poisonous atmosphere.

In April 1969 the late Terence O'Neill broadcast a speech of resignation from the premiership of Northern Ireland, where he said:

"Here we are, in this small country of ours, Protestant and Catholic, committed by history to live side by side. No solution based on the ascendancy of any section of our community can hope to endure. Either we live in peace, or we have no life worth living. For too long we have been torn and divided. Ours is called a Christian country. We could have enriched our politics with our Christianity, but far too often we have debased our Christianity with our politics. We seem to have forgotten that love of neighbour stands beside love of God as a fundamental principle of our religion."

So far I have spoken of the sickness: the sickness of sectarianism, the sickness of terrorism, the sickness of violence. Is there an antidote? I suspect that fear and suspicion and hatred of "the other" may be conditions as complex as cancers, and that no universally effective remedy may be available. But my agonising exposure to the problems of victims in Northern Ireland has given me much food for thought about possible remedies there. Of course we all want a "peace process" which works and which will endure. This is not, I believe, synonymous with a political process. Changes in constitutions and institutions and laws can be remarkably ineffective unless and until they are underpinned by changes in the hearts of men.

How are such changes to be sought? We are not likely to see some great ecumenical reconciliation which renders all previous differences irrelevant. But first we need to make a much greater effort to know and understand what the beliefs and practices of "the other" really are. I grew up in the Anglican tradition, was baptised into the Church of England and confirmed in the Church of Ireland. It was, I confess, a long time before I ever set foot in a Catholic church, and a great many of my co-religionists, I state with confidence, have never done so. They are free to imagine strange and unfamiliar mysteries taking place in exotic surroundings. This impression is soon dispelled if one attends, for example, a service at one of the fine modern Catholic churches designed in the north west of Ulster by the distinguished architect Liam McCormick. The simplicity and austerity of these places of worship is far removed from the baroque splendours of middle Europe. The service itself will be friendly and cheerful. Handshakes will be exchanged with the neighbour in the pew. Stripped of its disguise of Latinity, much of the order of service will have a familiar resonance to a practising Anglican.

And what does the Catholic in his own homogeneous community know or understand of the richness and variety of Protestant practice—whether it is reflected in the splendour and dignity of St Anne's Cathedral, in the boisterous enthusiasm of Methodist hymn-singing, or in the uprightness and spirituality of the best Presbyterian practice?

Not all walls are built, as the Berlin wall was built, of brick or stone. Rather do we build an invisible wall of stereotypes; the dour and humourless Protestant, the feckless and irresponsible Catholic. Because of this I find jokes based around ethnic or religious characteristics ultimately unfunny.

The corollary of a willingness to learn more about "the other" must be an eagerness to make the visitor from across the divide most warmly welcome. I would not like to suggest for a moment that there are no efforts on foot to achieve this. The Dean of the Anglican Cathedral of St Anne and the Administrator of the Catholic Cathedral of St Peter organise and encourage joint services and many other common ventures. Recently when a new Dean was installed at St Anne's, it was his Catholic neighbour and partner at St Peter's who embraced him with particular and noticeable warmth. These symbols are of great value.

Yet, while I am deeply conscious of all the theological difficulties and objections, I yearn for the day when this deepening of understanding can be carried a significant stage further. I know, as it happens, the current President of Ireland, Mary McAleese, quite well. She worked as an academic lawyer at Queen's University of Belfast, and I know her to be a particularly loyal and devout Roman Catholic. I found it deeply saddening that when, in a generous and touching gesture of inclusiveness, she took Holy Communion in a Church of Ireland Cathedral, her actions were censured and rebuked by the Catholic Archbishop of Dublin.

As a frequent and enthusiastic traveller I have often sat through wonderful services in some of the great Catholic cathedrals of Europe, in places like Avignon, Prague and Budapest. And I have on such occasions felt drawn to join with others—people who speak a different language and practice a different mode of religion—in full acceptance of the "body of Christ". Yes, of course, many important things still divide us, albeit few lay people really understand what these are. But cannot we find, must we not find the utmost demonstrable means to show that what unites us outweighs by far what divides us?

All of this brings me, inevitably, to the question of education. I can still remember in the early Seventies having to brief the then Prime Minister of Northern Ireland for an encounter with the Cardinal Archbishop of Armagh. I was at pains to point out that it was not just in Northern Ireland, but around the world, that the Catholic Church preferred wherever possible to see its young educated in a Catholic environment. It has to be said, too, that a great many Protestants where I live are very happy that the State schools, where de jure are open to all, are de facto almost exclusively Protestant in character. But the hard truth, I believe, is that the systems of separate education have failed in a most crucial particular. Their maintenance can only be justified by proven ability to inculcate, alongside academic knowledge, the most basic of Christian principles. Many high-principled teachers in both State and Church systems certainly strive to do so. The state encourages a progressive development of religiously integrated education, which nevertheless caters for a minority of children. All schools pursue a course of study bearing the acronym ECU, "education for mutual understanding". If there is such a striking failure in teaching our people to love one another as is demonstrated by recent events in Belfast I believe churchmen and public men need to think again about how our wounded community can ever be healed.

I am very proud to be a former pupil of a remarkable Belfast school, the Royal Belfast Academical Institution, founded in 1810 to be both school and college of higher education, prior to the establishment of the Queen's colleges in Ireland. In February 1814, at the opening of the Institution, a celebrated Belfast figure of the day, Dr William Drennan, spoke of

"the establishment of such societies of liberal and ingenious men, uniting in their labours, without regard to nation, sect or party, in one grand pursuit, alike interesting to all, by which mental prejudice may be worn off, a humane and truly philosophic spirit may be cherished in the heart as well as the head, in practice as well as theory.

"The Directors in their choice of masters and in their admission of scholars are perfectly unbiased by religious distinctions. They have sought for teachers, either in this or the other kingdom, wherever best recommended by their merits and experience in their professional departments, and by their morals and manners in their personal characters. Of nothing are the boards more desirous that that pupils of all religious denominations should communicate, by frequent and friendly intercourse, in the common business of education, by which means a new light might be given to the national character and habits, and all the children of Ireland should know and love each other."

The antidote to terrorism is not laws or constitutions or armies or doctrines, but love.

Just over a week later I was called upon to speak again in a great church, this time at a service in St Anne's Cathedral in Belfast to remember victims of violence in Northern Ireland. Not for the first time, I urged the appointment of a permanent Commissioner or Ombudsman for victims, a recommendation of my 1998 report not implemented until 2008.

On 27 March 2007 I launched my next book, *A Tragedy of Errors: The Government and Misgovernment of Northern Ireland*, published by Liverpool University Press, in the splendid surroundings of the Canada Room at Queen's University. To my enormous pleasure Lord Eames, the outgoing Archbishop of Armagh and one of the outstanding Ulstermen of his generation, agreed to be guest speaker. I said that evening:

A Tragedy of Errors is a "Janus" of a book because it tries to look in both directions. It looks back to all the agonies endured over so many years in this place we call home. The facts, at least, are in most cases a matter of record, although from time to time new light is focused on dark places. I have not wanted to disclose anything known by me in my life as a public servant which is not already in the public domain. My object has rather been to offer judgments—I hope fairly—but without shrinking from criticism, not least of myself and my contemporaries. We are often slaves of the received wisdom of the time, and only appreciate in retrospect, with sadness and regret, how incomplete was our contemporary understanding. And I have tried to bring to bear both the experience of a senior official and earlier academic training as an historian.

Those of us who have been involved in a project of this kind will know full well that there comes a stage when the text has to be finalised while events move on. There have of course been important developments since my book went to print. While I forecast the possibility of some at least of them, I could not know whether or when they might occur. It is by chance rather than design that we meet today after an historic encounter at Stormont.

The reader will see that my book includes some frank criticism of the part played by individuals in our affairs. But I would draw your attention to my reminder that few of those personalities discussed here believed at the time their actions were for other than the greater good. Yet I am one of those who do not believe that "the end justifies the means" and perhaps at least some of those whose ends have been transparent may reflect upon the justification offered for the means they chose to use. A more liberal use of the simple word "sorry" can do a great deal to buttress the high-flown language of the Good Friday and St Andrew's agreements, and I was glad to note the tone of some of the remarks made by the protagonists yesterday.

I have felt obliged to criticise some of the actions if not the motives of those I continue in other respects to admire. Has there ever been a British Prime Minister more articulate than Tony Blair, or more prepared to recognise Northern Ireland as a high national priority, meriting and receiving an immense amount of his time and attention? He has been an essential animator of the "peace process". The prize—the end of mass murder and brutal thuggery—has been great, but the cost of that prize has been very high. Political opinion in the province has been driven from the centre ground towards the more extreme exponents of unionism and nationalism in a community still not at peace with itself.

For his patience, perseverance and courage John Hume has earned his Nobel Peace Prize, and to him more than anyone else is due the credit for the entrenchment of the "consent principle", based on the democratic decision of voters across Ireland. But these achievements have also had their cost. It may indeed have been the case that the only argument for "cessation" likely to be acceptable to Sinn Féin was that there were better ways than violence to advance the cause of a united Ireland. Yet I fear the relationship between Hume and Adams at a critical time risked prejudicing the future of the SDLP as a wholly peaceful and democratic alternative to Sinn Féin, increased the sense of beleaguerment within the unionist community and drove them from more moderate politics into the strong arms of Ian Paisley.

The reader may guess that I am unlikely to offer myself as a DUP candidate, although I have had good reason in recent times to appreciate that the party can be an effective ally in the promotion of common causes. While its rhetoric in earlier days may possibly have inspired others to use unacceptable methods, it has earned the right to be viewed as a peaceful, constitutional and democratic organisation, and one of the gross errors made by many was to underestimate the powers and persistence of its leader.

As I looked back over the years to 1920, the question in my mind was: "Could the later explosion of violence, with all its tragic consequences, have been avoided?" I was drawn to ask this question above all by my experiences as Victims Commissioner in 1997/98 and as a current Commissioner for the Location of Victims' Remains. I and my own family, albeit targeted, were amongst the fortunate. We lost bricks and mortar, books and paintings, not life or limb. But these duties brought me into close and emotional contact with the disabled, the mourning relatives, and those who still do not have a body to bury or a grave to visit. The cover photograph of my book records the day in 1998 when I launched my report *We Will Remember Them*. Before going up to Stormont I cut from a local hedgerow a sprig of gorse, as a symbol of thorns and suffering, blossom and rebirth.

Was it all avoidable? My answer is a resounding "yes". We have witnessed, indeed, a real tragedy of errors. By 1920 partition was inevitable. Politicians in London must have known that that they were establishing in Northern Ireland a jurisdiction in which one faction would always be in power and another always in opposition. Parliament incorporated in the 1920 Act some notional safeguards against discrimination which proved to be relatively toothless, but they also provided in Section 75 that ultimate authority would be reserved to the supreme national Parliament at Westminster. Such was the reluctance to use that power or to threaten the use of it that by the 1960s some local politicians regarded it as a dead letter, and its use as unconstitutional.

Meanwhile the devolved institutions behaved in an entirely predictable way. There were at various times wise and generous men in Stormont cabinets who could see the need for more generosity to the minority community, and the dangers in failing to afford it. Yet the wider Unionist Party and its adherents regarded any modest move away from total control as an admission of the barbarian through the gates. Nor did the policy and posture of successive Irish governments in the Free State and Republic diminish this siege mentality, let alone promote the possibility of patient and unforced organic closeness.

However, my book attempts to look forward—always a hazardous exercise—as well as back. After yesterday it would be tempting to conclude that Northern Ireland in now "home and dry"; that peace is firmly rooted; that former gunmen and bombers have been transmuted into convinced democrats; that a coalition of the major parties will now move forward in amity and mutual respect towards the broad, sunlit uplands. I do not discount the possibility of a transition from insurgency to democracy. In their respective times and places, many contemporaries regarded Mandela and De Valera as the personifications of physical force. But such a transition can take time to be effective and convincing, and is more readily achieved where the former adversaries are nevertheless agreed on the definition of their nationality. Of course I wish our potential devolved ministers well, but the agreement to come together represents not an end but a beginning.

In principle I have always been an enthusiastic supporter of the concept of devolution. It is absurd and humiliating to find ourselves governed by a party which does not receive or invite a single vote from the people of Northern Ireland. Ministers imposed upon us can enforce with apparent relish initiatives clearly unwanted by local people. Of course some of these measures which we dislike may prove to be a "cruel necessity" even in the context of devolution, since it remains the fact that we will still need the goodwill of HM

Treasury to balance our books. The availability of a real stimulus to economic growth remains obscure.

For me, though, the real question is not whether devolution is desirable—for I firmly believe it is—but whether in the current polarised state of our politics it can provide a fair, reliable, stable and coherent system of government. If you go to the Public Record Office on Balmoral Avenue you can read for yourself the conclusions of the power-sharing Executive of 1974, now in the public domain; and you will see there that one of its first decisions was to operate on the basis of collective responsibility. Without acceptance of that principle there can be no coherence in the direction of government, no long-term stability. Yet if a new government of Northern Ireland operates on this basis, where will common ground be found on such issues as the nature and extent of North/South co-operation or on domestic issues such as the future of post-primary education? We will have to wait and see.

When the Sinn Féin leaders entered the meeting to secure endorsement of support for policing and justice, some shouted "traitor" at them. Some may, I suppose, shout "traitor" at me when I acknowledge that a united Ireland one day is more likely than not. In theory, though, it could happen at some future time when a narrow majority in Northern Ireland vote for something towards which a very large minority remains wholly antipathetic. That would be a tragic and disastrous outcome. It would simply import into a larger jurisdiction the awful divisions which have plagued us all these years. At the Merriman Summer School some years ago, I argued that those who purported to seek Irish unity had gone a most perverse way about it.

A few weeks ago I was asked to address a group from some 15 countries around the world about our situation, and in the later question period I was asked why Northern Ireland could not go independent. I said what I believed, that full independence would be fundamentally unviable both in financial and communitarian terms. I hope and pray that stable, lasting and effective devolution may be achieved, in spite of all my fears and reservations. But if this possibly last chance of limited government of ourselves were to prove unworkable, we who live here would need to think long and hard about the best means to live with some dignity and self-respect.

In conclusion, I want to give this first copy of my book to my dear wife Elizabeth, who confronted the worst of times with courage and has sustained me, throughout a long marriage, in everything I have tried to do. She shares the dedication with our children Caroline and Timothy, and my hope and prayer is that they will see our native province the peaceful and flourishing place we all wish it to be.

The publication of this book led to invitations to speak at various literary "summer schools" in such places as Armagh, Bangor and Scotland's "book town", Wigtown (where a fellow speaker was Marista Leishman, daughter of John Reith, founder of the BBC). A significant invitation came from the Merriman Summer School in County Clare. I had previously spoken there in 1997, and now I was asked to join in a session with a very distinguished Irish retired diplomat, Noel Dorr, who had been Irish Ambassador at the United Nations, Irish Ambassador in London and, for some eight years, Secretary of the Department of External Affairs. Wisely or unwisely, I decided to plunge into the turbulent waters of British/Irish and North/South relationships. Some aspects of what I said proved controversial, but in most cases represented a knee-jerk reaction to extracts published in newspapers. I welcome an opportunity to publish the text in full, and stand by the argument I advanced for more clarity of thinking about broad concepts of developing relationships. I said this:

Ten years have passed since I last had the privilege of speaking at the Merriman Summer School, held that year in Ennistymon. In 1997 speakers were asked to reflect on the way in which Ireland—that is to say the Free State and the successor Republic—had used three quarters of a century of independence. It was a gesture of open-mindedness, of a wish and ability to hear and reflect on disparate views, to invite me to deliver a "Northern perspective"; or at any rate a perspective from that community in the North not so far convinced of the benefits of sharing that independence. Any of you who were present on that occasion may remember that I was introduced by

Martin Mansergh, a man whose part in our relationship over many years has been striking.

Earlier this year, in a book entitled *A Tragedy of Errors*, I tried to explain the parts played in our decades-long tragedy by three groups of interests: the Parliament and Government of the United Kingdom; the institutions of the Free State and Republic; and the parties and communities in Northern Ireland itself. Every party or interest made errors with fateful consequences over the decades. I was myself certainly amongst them. I have sought in my book and elsewhere to admit to acts of omission or commission attributable to myself, my contemporaries and my tradition. Those who wish to be part of the solution do well to reflect that they may also have been part of the problem. All the protagonists in Northern Ireland made grievous mistakes. Above all, Westminster made the cardinal error of retaining an ultimate authority which it cravenly failed to exercise until we stood on the brink of calamity.

However in 1997 I was asked specifically to consider the stance of the Free State and Republic in addressing the question of the North. I then said this (and repeated it in my recent book):

"When an area and a community have long been embodied in another state to which they do not want to belong, it is perhaps inevitable that the first thrust of independence is to emphasise and encourage distinctiveness. This is particularly so when the jurisdiction enjoying a new-found independence is very much smaller in scale than that jurisdiction from which it has separated itself. It is understandable that the mere act of severance needs to be reinforced by emphatic statements of separate identity, from repainting the letter-boxes or issuing newly-designed stamps to matters of greater pith and substance. Even along as civilised a frontier as that between the United States and Canada, there is inevitably a certain wariness on the Canadian side, flowing from a perception of the overwhelming power and influence of the southern neighbour. The trouble here in Ireland, I would argue, was a schizophrenia of aspiration. The founding fathers of the State wished to see it free, independent and united—that is to say including within its embrace all the people on the island of Ireland. The new State demonstrated and asserted its new independence by policies and gestures of what one might call 'non-Britishness', a state not always easily distinguished from 'anti-Britishness'. But if you accept that it was a sense of 'Britishness' which, in part at least, characterised the 'separated brethren' of the North, then it was rather as if one cried 'Come and join us on the other side', while at the same time hacking down a good many of the existing bridges."

On 31 August 1997 the first leader in the *Irish Times* noted that in my Merriman talk three days before I had characterised much previous policy towards Northern Ireland as "deeply flawed, unproductive or even counter-productive". "Supposing there were, one day, a Northern majority in favour of unity, he asked, what intellectual preparation had been made for that contingency?" And the leader went on to quote my words: "Is it supposed the preoccupations of the distinctive Northern Unionist-Protestant community would just fade away? Is it imagined that the arrangements for the governance of a pretty homogeneous State would be apt for a new and heterogeneous one?" The article concluded by envisaging a successful conclusion to the "peace process". "A challenge," it argued, "of historic proportions will then face this government and indeed the people of this State. There are not too many signs of our preparedness."

Now we are ten years on from these remarks. I am ten years older if not wiser. Not least I have a clearer view of who I am, and a less settled view of who I choose to be. Only last year I unearthed fascinating detail about my great-great-grandfather, George William Bloomfield. He had been born, like generations of Bloomfields, in Suffolk in 1828, enlisted in the Royal Artillery, and by 1850 was a member of the garrison of the fort on Scattery Island in the mouth of the Shannon. There he met and married a local girl, Bridget McMahon, my County Clare great-great-grandmother. His first son in a large family, born in Ireland, was another George Bloomfield, my great-grandfather. I am fortunate enough to have a photograph, taken about 1900, of my then infant father with the three previous male generations. The oldest of these, a venerable figure with an impressive beard (albeit younger at the time than I am now) is that very George William who fell in love on Scattery Island and gave me a County Clare great-great-grandmother.

Last year, after this moving discovery, I drove from my home in County Down to Kilrush and took the ferry to Scattery, now uninhabited. I walked in an abandoned graveyard with monuments to long-dead McMahons, to reflect on centuries upon centuries of Christian worship and piety in this beautiful place with its round tower, ruined churches, holy well and Ogham stone. From the highest point of the island I could look down to the site of the old battery and the adjacent lighthouse. And so it was that I discovered, well into the eighth decade of my life here in Ireland, that I—the son of parents who crossed from England in 1929 and never wanted to return—am not, after all, just one of the "blow-ins" from "across the water", but that I can link across that other water, the fabled water of the majestic Shannon, with still older generations yet unknown to me who worshipped in ancient churches and looked for cures at holy wells.

If my perception of myself has changed since I last spoke at the Merriman, so has my perception of Ireland. The Republic continues to surf the tide of prosperity and development. Indeed I read in the London *Times* the other day that the average wealth per head of citizens of the Republic is now the second highest in the world. Ireland punches well above its weight in the European Community. The peaceful aspirations for Northern Ireland being expressed in 1997 have at last been realised, with an opportunity, if not a total assurance, of stable and enduring domestic government there. While the North continues to rely very heavily on British Exchequer support, there is a growing sense of the need to be more self-sufficient. A confident Republic, looking with confidence to its own welfare and destiny, no longer needs or displays that excessive degree of "distancing" from the neighbour island which I identified ten years ago. Ireland versus England at Croke Park had the right result, and not just in terms of the number of points scored. On the other hand, that old bogey-man, England, now has to cope with ever more assertive regimes in Edinburgh and Cardiff as well as Belfast.

It is a special pleasure to share a platform today with Noel Dorr, a most distinguished diplomat and public servant, with whom in my own official life it was always a joy, and often a learning experience, to deal. I found in Noel and the great Ken Whitaker and Dermot Nally and Dermot Gallagher people with whom I could discuss issues honestly, and if necessary in confidence. I recall, for instance, visiting the State Department in Washington in double harness with Dermot Gallagher to negotiate what would become the International

Fund for Ireland, an act of generosity led by the United States which has poured many millions of dollars, pounds or euros into Northern Ireland and the Border counties. One day I arrived at "Foggy Bottom", the headquarters of the State Department, to find a red carpet rolled out at the entrance. This seemed an extravagantly flattering gesture until I learned that another visitor to State that day was a certain Mr Gorbachov, from a place well to the east of Lisdoonvarna. This mission was a prime example of the mutual benefit of working together for a common cause.

More recently I attended a moving event in Dublin; a funeral mass for the former Tanaiste, John Wilson. We had first encountered each other as the respective Victims Commissioners on either side of the Border. Thereafter we were jointly appointed by the two governments to lead an Independent Commission for the Location of Victims' Remains, a poignant task which still continues, and in which I am now joined by Frank Murray, a former Secretary to the government. John Wilson was a man of many parts; scholar, teacher, linguist, politician, sportsman; and as his coffin was carried from the church they laid upon it, over the tricolour, the football shirt of the county for which he and his team-mates had won the Sam Maguire at the New York Polo Grounds in 1947.

I want, though, to return to the theme of my talk at Ennistymon in 1997. How do I see events developing in Northern Ireland from this time forward, and in what if any circumstances can I envisage a different and much closer form of association between the two jurisdictions in Ireland?

The coming-together of political factions for so long totally antipathetic to each other was an extraordinary and striking event. It may even have been historic; as to that history in due course will make its own judgement. On that memorable day at Stormont as the new administration assumed office, my wife and I were far away in Lisbon, the Portuguese capital, but were able to follow the events on BBC World and CNN, and read about the new dispensation in the local and Spanish newspapers. This settlement in our tiny province was a source of world interest and a stimulus to hope, compromise and renewed effort in other divided societies.

It is, of course, wonderful that we no longer live under the shadow or threat of daily violence, and I wish the participating parties—

whatever their previous records and attitudes—every success as they set about their daunting task. With the low-key ending of the so-called "Operation Banner" the British army in the North now recedes into the background of training and preparation for other actual or potential conflicts in a troubled world. On the positive side, the very obvious efforts of former bitter enemies to treat each other with respect are very striking, and it should be said that Bertie Ahern has played a significant part in this. As someone who was inside Stormont Castle waiting for Jack Lynch as Ian Paisley bombarded him with snowballs, I had to pinch myself as I watched those amicable encounters at Government Buildings or on the Boyne.

Yet of course the real test is not the test of forming a government; it is the more stringent test of making it work for the benefit of everyone. And, since Northern Ireland has no armed forces or foreign policy, there are huge areas of domestic affairs where common ground is readily available. All the parties and all the people of Northern Ireland would like to ride on the back of the economic tiger; all want more inward investment, more jobs, more prosperity, more emphasis on research and development. Envious eyes have turned across the Border towards your low rate of Corporation Tax, and our politicians and businessmen, with help and encouragement from friends here, have sought to persuade the Treasury that a lower rate in Northern Ireland is indispensable as a vital stimulus to economic growth. I wish this campaign every success. I aimed at this target years ago when I was Permanent Secretary at the Department of Economic Development, and was blocked by fears of profit manipulation by firms operating both inside and outside Northern Ireland.

On the other hand we have to recognise that the Northern Ireland Executive, bringing together the DUP, Sinn Féin, the UUP and the SDLP, is not a conventional government, and may indeed be unique in the world. In recent years people have become very familiar with patterns of coalition government, and indeed there are many countries in Europe and further afield in which coalition is a commonplace. Typically, though, the largest party will choose a partner or partners at the conclusion of a negotiating and bargaining process, designed to produce a broad programme for government, or al least a series of principles, by which all participants can stand.

In Northern Ireland, under the arrangements set in place by the Good Friday and St Andrew's Agreements, there is no need for such a process. Participation in government flows solely from the number of seats won, rather than from any search for common ground. In one sense one can say this is very democratic. I have long been interested in the Swiss federal system, where it has long been recognised that any government failing to acknowledge the main ethnic and linguistic groups would lack stability and universal legitimacy. But those now joined together in Northern Ireland have for most of their careers experienced only the politics of opposition. Within those politics, it is all too easy to accumulate a wish-list rather than face the difficult, frustrating and potentially divisive business of prioritisation. And of course we in Northern Ireland have spending powers but no tax-raising powers. I still recall with a degree of dismay my role in 1974 as Secretary to the all too short-lived "power-sharing Executive". They had, indeed, agreed on a purported "programme for government", but it was in my judgement a programme completely detached from financial and funding reality. That government did not last long enough to hit the buffers.

I was trained to be a Cabinet or Government Secretary, but found myself after the debacle of 1974 an admiral without a ship. But I have made a deep study of systems of government, which leads me to emphasize the centrality of the concept of collective responsibility. Unless this is accepted, government will prove sooner or later to be a fragmentation bomb. In the case of Northern Ireland, the relevant constitutional Agreements impose a requirement of consensus as the Executive and Assembly face contentious issues. This requirement presents no problems where there is a high degree of mutual interest. Who will not fight for more jobs, more affordable housing, and a more self-reliant economy, a better-trained and educated workforce? Yet even in these domestic areas, there continue to be matters which are, or could prove to be, divisive. Let me give an example. About half the members of the Executive favour the retention of our grammar schools and some acceptable basis of academic selection as a criterion for entry. Others regard any form of academic selection as socially divisive and counter-productive. In such a contentious area, with strongly held views at stake, consensus will not be easily achieved.

But of course the settlement as a whole does not just deal with the internal governance of Northern Ireland. With the restoration of devolution, both the "East/West" institutions, bringing North and South of Ireland together with England, Scotland, Wales, the Channel Islands and the Isle of Man, and the "North/South" institutions, bringing together ministers from North and South, have been re-activated and re-energised. It is clear to me that Sinn Féin in particular will tolerate the symbolism of East/West encounters for the opportunity they see in North/South encounters to promote the cause of Irish unity.

Irish unity. Here we come to the heart of the matter. What does this "Irish unity" so often spoken of and advocated mean? The mechanism for institutional unity is clear. If and when a majority of the people living in Northern Ireland vote in favour of such a step, legislation will be introduced into the parliaments of the two sovereign states to transfer the six counties from the one jurisdiction to the other. I do not, myself, believe that such a vote is likely any time soon; probably not in my lifetime, even if you invite me to a third Merriman after another ten years.

The views of people in the Republic about the desirability in principle of such an outcome are clear. If the assumption is of a peaceful, non-divisive and affordable transition, who here is likely to say "nay" to it? But I suggest that there are fundamental issues which need to be addressed by politicians and others here in the South well before any imminent prospect of unity looms large. What kind of a united Irish state would it be? Would the degree of inevitable change in the Irish polity be acceptable? Would the economic and financial consequences of unity be acceptable both in the six and the twenty-six counties?

What kind of a united Irish state would it be? Might it involve federalism or devolution or other means of institutional protection for certain rights and interests? Would Belfast, a capital city for more than eight decades already, with its legislature, law courts, its pride in being "no mean city", recede into the status of just another provincial town, or would a new and more diverse Ireland disperse and share its sovereign national institutions?

Then there is the question of inevitable change in the Irish polity itself. What a blessing it is, in our turbulent modern world, to live in a pretty homogeneous society. As Shia fights Sunni in Iraq, as Arab fights Jew in Israel or Palestine, as China oppresses Buddhist Lamaism in Tibet, I reflect upon the benefits you have enjoyed in these 26 counties from being a society with a common heritage, with religious activities, sports and games, language and culture which, to some degree at least, nearly all of you share. I contrast all of this with the Northern Ireland in which I have lived since 1931. If my old school, RBAI, founded in 1810 by William Drennan, one of the Presbyterian United Irishmen, wants to play rugby with a Catholic school, it has to look to Blackrock or Belvedere rather than its Belfast neighbour, St Malachy's. From our school every year boys move on to a host of universities in England or Scotland. Of course the Republic itself is today changing rapidly. Some count 200,000 Poles around Greater Dublin; but at least these immigrants have an affinity with the predominant Catholic faith. An Ireland embracing in both senses of the word a million Protestants would be, and would have to be, a very different place. I have to say, though, that the question of religion looms much less large today than it did when I was young. There was a very real perception of the Irish Republic as a theocratic State. Those days are now over. Let us think of the prospect of ultimate unity or a changed relationship as a process, not a single dramatic step. Let us rather think of it as a possible or potential contract between distinct groups of people, with all the cards on the table. The process of which I speak should have a modest beginning and no predetermined end. It should emphasize encounter, the development of mutual trust and movement only by general agreement. We now have in operation a range of North-South bodies which in the nature of things will involve politicians and civil servants in working together, getting to know each other, getting—I hope and believe—to trust each other. We all know that Sinn Féin's paramount priority is to achieve Irish unity as rapidly as possible. I would say two things to them, as someone who accepts their presence in government in spite of republican efforts to kill me years ago. John Hume was quite right to say consistently over many years that the only unity worth having would be a unity of people, not of territories. What possible benefit would it be to import into a still relatively homogeneous Irish state a welter of unresolved differences? Let the Ministerial Council, let the North-South bodies address topics strictly on their merits, pursue issues unarguably for mutual benefit and avoid at all costs a backlash from those disposed to regard the whole thing as a Trojan horse. Sinn Féin reminds us, and fairly reminds us, that it is for them a big step to sit down as members of a devolved government within a continuing British jurisdiction. But please appreciate, too, that for the DUP it is a big step to play a constructive part in North-South institutions; to embrace Bertie both literally and metaphorically.

May I digress for a moment on the subject of the Taoiseach? Away back in the Nineties my wife and I were staying at the Royal Crescent Hotel in Bath, as it happens a week after a meeting of European Finance Ministers in that beautiful city. For the chambermaids, the waitresses, and the porters only one of these political personalities had registered. "That Mr Ahern, what a lovely man." Whatever Charlie Haughey may or may not have said about him, he seems to me an outstanding example of the impact and benefit of human warmth in political and diplomatic negotiations. When things are tough and disagreement surrounds you, it makes a difference if people actually like you. I myself have had only one encounter of any length with him. It was 1998, and I had produced my report as Victims Commissioner, *We Will Remember Them*. I had the opportunity to brief the Taoiseach at Government Buildings in what I expected to be a brief but civil encounter. Instead I was made to feel like a friend who had dropped in for an amicable chat.

If Irish unity at some stage begins to look like the outcome of a popular vote in the North, it is essential that the parties to any hypothetical transfer of sovereignty should fully understand the financial and economic implications and costs. The standard of living and level of wealth on the northern side of the Border have fallen behind those in the Republic. With "the Troubles" hopefully behind us there should be great economic potential in the North, and the possibility of very substantial investment, particularly if the North were to be embodied in a favourable corporate tax regime. Yet on the other side of the equation there is the reality that Northern Ireland enjoys even its present level of economic activity and public services only with the benefit of massive annual transfers from the British Exchequer.

This issue last raised its head in the setting of Garret Fitzgerald's New Ireland Forum. I have offered a critical judgement on the work of that Forum in *A Tragedy of Errors*. I commented: "Although the report went on to express an openness to 'other views which may contribute to political development', unionist reaction was understandably focused on the preference for a unitary state and the prospect of alternative options as mere staging posts en route to that objective. Moreover, in its analysis of the underlying political, historical, cultural and socio-economic backgrounds, the Forum had significantly failed to take adequate cognisance of strong arguments advanced by economists that it would be financially impossible for a unitary Irish state to maintain existing standards of public services in Northern Ireland. And although the report was charged with concern to preserve the rights and distinctive ethos of the Protestant and unionist majority in Northern Ireland (and prospective minority in a united Ireland), it appeared to characterise that ethos as Protestant rather than British." Summing up, I conclude that "everything about unionists was to be respected, with the exception of their unionism".

Let us stay for the moment with the economic and financial issues. Of course the Republic is a much more prosperous place today than it was when the Forum reported in 1984. Yet some fundamental questions remain unanswered or even unaddressed. What would be the costs falling to be borne by the Irish Exchequer in the event of a pattern of Irish unity guaranteeing no reduction in the standard of services and benefits in Northern Ireland? Would the consequence of such a guarantee be an increase in the burden of taxation currently borne by taxpayers in the Republic, and an increase from British tax levels in the North? Or would there have to be recourse to substantial borrowing for an extended transitional period? Would the British government of the day, in light of shedding a continuing indefinite burden, ease the transition by some kind of tapering "dowry"? (I may say that I heard this canvassed at a conference years ago, and drawing gales of sceptical laughter from a very senior English bureaucrat). If these costs were fully investigated and openly revealed, would all those concerned be willing to meet them? We have before us, I would remind you, the history of Germany since the removal of the Wall and the collapse of communism. The assimilation of the former DDR has proved neither easy nor inexpensive.

I believe the New Ireland Forum side-stepped some vital issues. I have just discussed one of these, the question of financial viability and acceptability. Another, as I have argued in my book, is the willingness to acknowledge and respect "Britishness". Please do not suppose that if, in some future poll, 50.1% of the electorate were to vote for Irish unity, the outvoted 49.9% would tramp into the new jurisdiction like a defeated army. Successive Stormont governments were far too slow to acknowledge that the sense of "Irishness" felt by such an extensive minority in their midst could not be suppressed or ignored, but ought to be recognised and respected. Now, belatedly, institutional links, support for Irish language and culture, the universal acceptance and recognition of Irish passports go some way to indicate that "Irishness" is alive and well beyond the territory of the Republic. Let us imagine a time when the boot could be on the other foot. Triumphalists may take the line "We are the masters now. Let these crypto-Brits recognise that henceforth their loyalty is to Ireland, and only to Ireland." From those who in the past have too often felt oppressed and under-valued such a reaction would be understandable, but nevertheless unwise and a disservice to a new Ireland.

I offer you my very personal perspective. My oldest identifiable ancestors, from the place called Blonville, travelled across the Channel in the aftermath of the Norman Conquest. They came, over time, to congregate in East Anglia, particularly in Suffolk. My father, under age, joined the Royal Flying Corps in the Great War. I am—and am proud to be—a graduate of Oxford University, an Honorary Fellow of my old college, and a Knight of the Order of the Bath. Yet, as I grow older, I care less and less which flag is flown and which anthem played where I live. I am very comfortable, if it endures, with an indefinitely prolonged situation in which local politicians will effectively govern Northern Ireland, with the main English intervention an invaluable continuing subsidy. But I do not think I could bear, with any sense of self-respect, a further relapse into that parody of democratic government described as "direct rule", under which we lived for so many increasingly humiliating years. We have been governed by a party which had not received or even invited a single vote from the people of Northern Ireland. We have had our laws whisked through the British parliament with a minimum of debate and no opportunity for amendment. We have been made to feel peculiarly unloved by many of those to whom we have pledged our loyalty for generations. So it is that I do not find the idea of some form of Irish unity or closer association—almost certainly after my time—in any way unthinkable in principle. But what is conceivably acceptable in principle would have to be mutually acceptable in practice. Far-sighted politicians, economists and academics will have to think long and hard about the true nature, cost, ethos and dynamics of a new orientation of affairs. No crude majority vote could or should ignore or eliminate a continuing sense of "Britishness" likely to be retained by many people. How might this be done?

And so I return to the preference for process over predetermined conclusion. Let Catholic and Protestant, unionist and republican, learn in the first instance to work harmoniously together in the North for the public good rather than for ulterior motives. Let North and South co-operate over a widening range of issues, proceeding always on a basis of mutual consent. Let us acknowledge that, however dominant and oppressive that other island may have been in the past, today we should be the greatest and most natural of friends. Let us build on the foundations of our North-South and East-West institutions a commonwealth of common heritage and mutual understanding.

Just over a fortnight ago, as chairman of the Board at RBAI, I welcomed visitors to an event on our campus staged by Feile an Phobail, the West Belfast Festival. Sean McMahon, perhaps a remote relative of mine through my County Clare ancestors, spoke of the life of Robert Lynd, a celebrated son of the school, fluent Irish speaker, supporter of Home Rule and a brilliant essayist compared by some with Hazlitt.

When William Drennan spoke at the opening of the Institution in 1814, he used some eloquent words which I keep always in mind. "Of nothing," he said, "are the Boards more desirous than that pupils of all religious denominations should communicate ... in the common business of education, by which means a new turn might be given to the national character and habits, and all the children of Ireland should know and love each other." By the means of education, he told his audience, "you cannot perform a service more useful to your children, or more honorable, and at the same time profitable, to your native land. Here they were born, here let them be bred; and in their rising years let them be early accustomed (and what is education, but early custom?) to taste the sweetness of our native soil and to associate everything instructive, amiable, and endearing, with the words—OUR COUNTRY." Amen to that.

After forty years of discretion, I confess to having enjoyed the opportunity to express views of my own. In my old life I enjoyed access to ministers and the opportunity to make recommendations and suggestions to them. They might well decide to do something different, as was their prerogative. I played the game by its rules, and any disagreement while serving I kept to myself. Today I am a free citizen in a free country. I speak these days only for myself, and ask no more.

Index